Slow Cooker Meals
EASY HOME COOKING FOR BUSY PEOPLE

Mouth-Watering Family Favorites

Cajun-Style Meals,
plus Appetizers, Pastas,
Seafood, Meats, Soups, Stews,
Chili, and 17 Desserts...
all made in your Slow Cooker!

Cypress Cove
Publishing

by NEAL BERTRAND

ACKNOWLEDGEMENTS

I would like to thank all of the nice ladies associated with the LSU AgCenter and their members of the Volunteers for Family & Community (VFC) homemaker clubs across the state of Louisiana who contributed recipes and advice, and for their help in making this cookbook a success. In particular, Quincy Cheek, Rapides Parish; Mandy Armentor, Vermilion Parish; Connie Aclin, Caddo Parish; Elizabeth Lynn, Bienville Parish; Kathy Mauthe, Tangipahoa Parish – all with the LSU AgCenter.

I would also like to thank Cathy S. Judd, LSU AgCenter Lincoln Parish, for contributing a few recipes from her "Lunch and Learn" recipe booklet.

~~~~~~~~~~~~~~~~

Visit our website for new items and free recipes:
www.CypressCovePublishing.com & **www.BestSlowCookerMeals.com**

CYPRESS COVE PUBLISHING
ATTN: Neal Bertrand
P.O. Box 91626
Lafayette, LA 70509-1626

ISBN: 978-0-9705868-9-6

Library of Congress Control Number: 2010916034

ABOUT THE FRONT AND BACK COVER This beautiful, mouth-watering dish of Cajun Pepper Steak on the front cover is one of many meals that can be made in your slow cooker. Look for the recipe on page 34. On the back cover are Sausage Sauce Piquante and Peach Cobbler which can be found on pages 38 and 84, respectively.

AUTHOR, EXECUTIVE EDITOR AND PUBLISHER Neal Bertrand
FOOD STYLING AND COVER DESIGN Elizabeth Bell, eBell Design, Lafayette, La.
FRONT AND BACK COVER PHOTOGRAPHY Travis Gauthier, Zoom Photo Studio, Lafayette, La.
BOOK DESIGN AND PRODUCTION Jeremy Bertrand, Cypress Cove Publishing

CONTENTS

INTRODUCTION

In 2008, I wrote and published my second cookbook, *Rice Cooker Meals: Fast Home Cooking for Busy People.* I was so excited about cooking a one-pot meal in 30 minutes that I was spreading the word about my book, and it became very popular with busy people who still like to cook, as opposed to feeding their families fast food.

In the process of distributing my book around my home state of Louisiana, I met a lot of people who were fans of my book. They kept asking me questions that, at first, I found to be a little irritating, such as, "Will these rice cooker meal recipes work in my slow cooker?" "When are you coming out with a slow cooker meals cookbook?"

Initially, in my mind I scoffed at the idea. I thought to myself, *These people just don't understand! Here you have a Rice Cooker Meals cookbook where you can cook a one-pot meal in 30 minutes. Why would you want to cook the same thing that takes 8 hours?* I had a hard time with that at first.

Then I realized – wait a minute – they have a point here! Put the ingredients in the slow cooker pot, turn it on, and go to work and forget about it. When you get back home the food is ready to eat! That basically amounts to the same thing. Prepare the ingredients, put them in the pot and forget about it. Not only that, but I had a rude awakening when I found out that most people don't have a rice cooker. (*WHAT?* How can that be? Almost everyone in south Louisiana has a rice cooker! I grew up cooking rice on the stove, then the rice cooker came along, which was a major kitchen miracle, in my opinion.) However, more people own a slow cooker or Crock Pot. So, thanks to my friends and customers, this book has been birthed.

So, I wanted to find out if my *Rice Cooker Meals* recipes can be cooked in a slow cooker. Yes, I converted many of them to be cooked in a slow cooker; they are very delicious and appear within these pages.

I wanted to provide you with a lot of recipes, so I got help from homemaker clubs associated with the Louisiana State University (LSU) AgCenter. I asked these club members to submit their tested and proven recipes that are family favorites, and I present them to you within these pages.

Neal Bertrand, Author & Publisher
Cypress Cove Publishing
Lafayette, Louisiana, USA

FOREWORD

What the LSU AgCenter Ladies Have to Say

Working with the LSU AgCenter Cooperative Extension Service has taught me so much about the people of Louisiana, and one lesson in particular I learned recently has left me baffled. In south Louisiana (loosely defined as south of Alexandria) many families have, and use a rice cooker on a regular basis. North of Alexandria, rice cookers are scarce. It's rare to see them for sale at local discount stores in the northern part of the state. In central Louisiana – it's a sort of mixed territory. Some people have them, some people don't. I recently had some "Northerners" visiting my home in Lecompte, La., about 15 miles south of Alexandria. When they noticed my rice cooker on the counter they anxiously exclaimed, "Oh, I've never seen one of those in real life!"

Slow cookers are a whole different story – everybody has one and many people I know from all over the state use them on a regular basis. As a Family & Consumer Sciences Extension Agent, I get many requests for recipes for healthy, wholesome meals. Slow cooker recipes are always the most popular with clients. Slow cookers were first introduced to the general public in the early seventies, but the greatest advantage to using them still rings true today – about 15-20 minutes of preparation time in the morning yields a welcoming aroma when you walk in the door and a nutritious, tasty meal to enjoy with your family at the end of the day.

Many of the recipes provided in this book can be easily adjusted/modified to include less fat and sodium for healthier meals. There are many cookbooks out on the market for slow cooker recipes, but Neal does such a good job of focusing on recipes with Cajun "flair," that home cooks in Louisiana, and many other places, for that matter, want to provide for their families!

Quincy L. Cheek, M. Ed
Family & Consumer Sciences Agent – Nutrition
LSU AgCenter
Rapides Parish

Slow cookers have been around for numerous years. As a busy mom and wife who works outside of the home, the slow cooker is a life saver some days for me because before I leave I can put some food in the slow cooker, put it on COOK and by the time I come home a healthy, nutritious and delicious meal is cooked and ready to serve to my family. Slow cookers are available in numerous sizes and found at most retail outlets. They are convenient time-savers for busy families like mine, and a money saver.

This recipe book has recipes for all tastes and every type of meal you can imagine! Who would have thought after reviewing this book I can actually make desserts in the slow cooker. With this cookbook you are sure to find some new family favorites all while not breaking too much of a sweat over the stove. Enjoy cooking and trying the recipes in this book, because I know I can't wait to try some more recipes.

Thanks!

Mandy G. Armentor, MS, RD, LDN
Associate Extension Agent-FCS-Nutrition
Vermilion Parish Extension Service
Abbeville, La.

THE SLOW COOKER – A KITCHEN GENIE

Because of a busy schedule and a hectic lifestyle, Mom needs relief from heavy kitchen duty. Meals that are simple, light, nutritious and fast – especially fast – save her time without sacrificing her family's nutrition. Fortunately, saving on meal preparation time doesn't have to mean drive-through sandwiches, leftovers or frozen dinners.

Planning and organization do take an initial time investment but ultimately save more time in the kitchen.

Start by planning your meals, keeping in mind how much time you have for preparation. Then prepare a grocery list based on the meals you have planned. The better job you do of planning, the fewer trips you will make to the store, saving you both time and money.

One valuable tool that will help save you meal preparation time is the slow cooker. It's enjoying a resurgence in popularity these days as a new generation of cooks is discovering that it is a kitchen genie.

This countertop appliance cooks foods slowly at a low temperature, which means that vitamins and minerals are retained, less expensive cuts of meat are tenderized and meats shrink less. Your food cooks slowly all day while you are away, freeing you to concentrate on other priorities knowing that supper will be ready to serve when you arrive home.

Most cookers have at least two settings. The two heat settings on most cookers are low (200 degrees) and high (300 degrees). How long it takes for your food to cook depends on the setting you select.

To prevent scorching or sticking in the slow cooker, it is recommended that the lid be lifted occasionally. Every time the lid is lifted, add 20 minutes to the total cooking time.

To qualify as a safe slow cooker, the appliance must be able to cook slowly for unattended cooking, yet be out of the bacterial danger zone which is 40 to 140 degrees F. which is the optimum temperature for bacterial growth.

To test the safety of your slow cooker:

- Fill cooker with 2 quarts of water.
- Heat on LOW for eight hours or desired cooking time.
- Check the water temperature with an accurate food thermometer (do this quickly as the temperature drops 10-15 degrees when the lid is removed).
- The temperature of the water should be 185 degrees F. Temperatures *above* this would indicate that a product cooked for eight hours without stirring would be overdone. Temperatures *below* this may indicate the cooker does not heat high enough or fast enough to avoid potential food safety problems.

There are many recipes that are suitable for slow cookers, giving your family variety in their meals. Give a slow cooker as a gift or just give one to yourself to save you time for those busy days.

Connie Aclin
LSU AgCenter
Extension Educator

APPETIZERS

Bacon Cheese Dip

16 slices bacon (about 12 oz.), diced, fried and well drained

16 oz. cream cheese, cubed, room temperature

4 cups shredded cheddar cheese

1 cup half-and-half

2 tsp. Worcestershire sauce

1 tsp. dried minced onion

1/2 tsp. dry mustard

1/2 tsp. salt

Dash hot sauce

Put all ingredients in the slow cooker; cover and cook on LOW, stirring occasionally, for about 1 to 2 hours, until cheese is melted and mixture is hot. Taste and adjust seasonings, and keep on LOW to serve. Serve with cubed or sliced French bread or other dippers.

Cheese & Sausage Dip

1 (1 lb.) package Velveeta cheese

1 can chili (no beans)

1 lb. medium or spicy sausage, browned and crumbled

Combine cheese, chili, and sausage in slow cooker.
Put it in the slow cooker on LOW until blended and then keep it there to serve.
You can easily double the recipe.

Hot Spinach Cheese Dip

1 large package (16 to 20 oz.) frozen chopped spinach, thawed and squeezed dry
2 (8 oz.) packages cream cheese, cut in cubes
3/4 cup chopped green onion
1/2 tsp. garlic powder
1/4 tsp. coarsely ground black pepper
1/4 tsp. paprika
2 cups shredded cheddar cheese
1 can (8 oz.) water chestnuts, drained, chopped
Assorted crackers, chips, or vegetable dippers

In slow cooker, combine spinach and cream cheese. Add green onion, garlic powder, pepper, and paprika. Cover and cook on LOW for 2 hours, stirring once or twice, until very hot. Reserve 1/4 cup of shredded cheese for topping. Stir in the remaining cheese and water chestnuts. Sprinkle reserved cheese over top. Serve with chips, crackers, or vegetables for dipping.

Chili-Cheese Taco Dip

1 lb. ground beef
1 can chili (no beans)
1 lb. mild Mexican Velveeta cheese, cubed or shredded

Brown hamburger; drain well and transfer to slow cooker. Add chili and cheese; cover and cook on LOW until cheese is melted, about 1 to 1 1/2 hours, stirring occasionally to blend ingredients. Serve warm with tortilla chips.

Pizza Dip

1 lb. lean ground beef
2 cups pizza sauce
8 oz. grated cheddar cheese
8 oz. grated Mozzarella

1 tsp. dried leaf oregano
1/2 tsp. dried sweet basil
1 tbsp. cornstarch
Parmesan cheese, optional

Brown ground beef well; drain off fat. Combine ground beef with all other ingredients in the slow cooker. Cover and cook on LOW for 3 hours. If desired, add Parmesan cheese to taste. Serve with tortilla chips.

Crawfish & Crab Dip

1 stick butter, chopped
1 onion, chopped
1 jalapeno pepper, chopped
1 bell pepper, chopped
5 cloves garlic, minced
1/2 cup green onion tops, chopped
1/2 tsp. dried parsley flakes

TABASCO® Brand Pepper Sauce to taste, or serve at the table
1/2 cup water
1 lb. crawfish tails, peeled & deveined
12 to 16 oz. real or imitation crabmeat, chopped fine
1 cup processed cheese

Add all ingredients to slow cooker except seafood and cheese, stir well, cover and cook on LOW for 6 hours or more. Add seafood and cook on HIGH for one hour, then add cheese, stir until melted and serve.

Neal Bertrand
Lafayette, La.

Spicy Chicken Wings
in Barbecue Sauce

3 lbs. chicken wings (16 wings)
Salt and pepper, to taste
1 1/2 cups favorite barbecue sauce
1/4 cup honey

2 tsp. prepared mustard or
  spicy mustard
2 tsp. Worcestershire sauce
TABASCO® to taste, optional

Rinse chicken wings; pat dry. Cut off and discard wing tips then cut each wing at the joint to make two sections. Sprinkle wing pieces with salt and pepper; place wings on a lightly oiled broiler pan. Broil about 4 inches from the heat for 10 minutes on each side, or until chicken wings are nicely browned. Transfer chicken wings to slow cooker.
In a bowl, combine barbecue sauce, honey, spicy mustard, Worcestershire sauce, and TABASCO®. Pour sauce over chicken wings. Cover and cook on LOW for 4 to 5 hours or on HIGH 2 to 2 1/2 hours. Serve directly from slow cooker, keeping temperature on LOW. Makes about 30 chicken wings.

Ultimate Party Meatballs

1 (16-oz.) can jellied cranberry sauce
1 (12-oz.) bottle chili sauce

1 (2-lb.) bag frozen, pre-cooked,
  cocktail-size meatballs

Combine sauces and pour over meatballs in slow cooker. Cover and cook 4 hours on HIGH, or on LOW for 6 to 8 hours.

Makes 30 appetizer servings.

Helen Joyce M. Alleman
Rayne, La.

Turkey Meatballs

3 cups favorite barbecue sauce
2 cups apple jelly
2 to 3 tbsp. tapioca, (for thicker
    sauce), optional
2 tbsp. vinegar
2 eggs, beaten
1/2 cup dry bread crumbs, seasoned

1/4 cup milk
1/2 tsp. garlic powder
1/2 tsp. salt
1/2 tsp. onion powder
2 lbs. ground turkey
Non-stick vegetable spray

Stir together barbecue sauce, jelly, tapioca (if used), and vinegar in slow cooker. Cover and cook on HIGH while preparing meatballs. For meatballs, in large bowl combine egg, bread crumbs, milk, garlic powder, salt, and onion powder. Add ground turkey and mix well. Shape into 3/4-inch meatballs. Spray a 12-inch non-stick skillet with vegetable spray; add meatballs and brown on all sides over medium heat. Drain meatballs and add to slow cooker; stir very gently to coat with sauce. Cover and cook on HIGH for 1 1/2 to 2 hours. Makes about 5 dozen meatballs.

Spicy Chili Meatballs
in Barbecue Sauce

3 to 4 dozen small meatballs
1 (12 oz.) jar apple jelly
1 1/2 cups barbecue sauce
2 poblano chili peppers or Anaheim
    peppers, coarsely chopped
1/2 cup chopped onion

Dash garlic powder
1 tsp. chili powder
1/4 tsp. chipotle chili
    powder, optional
1/2 tsp. ancho chili powder,
    optional

Combine all ingredients in a 3 to 5-quart slow cooker. Cover and cook on LOW for 4 to 6 hours. Makes 3 to 4 dozen meatball appetizers, or serve with rice for a family meal. This recipe can easily be doubled for a bigger crowd.

MEATS & POULTRY

Sweet & Smokey Barbecue Pulled Pork Sandwiches

1 tbsp. vegetable oil
1 (3 1/2-lb.) boneless pork
    shoulder roast
1 tsp. salt
1/2 tsp. black pepper
1 cup chopped onion

1 (16-oz.) can jellied cranberry sauce
1 (12-oz.) bottle chili sauce
2 tbsp. minced chipotle peppers in
    adobo sauce or 1 tsp. cayenne
    pepper
12 to 16 hamburger buns; split

Heat oil in large skillet over medium-high heat. Season pork with salt and black pepper. Add pork to skillet and cook for 6 to 8 minutes or until browned on both sides. Place pork and onion in cooker and cover; cook on LOW for 7 to 9 hours or until meat is tender.

Remove pork and onion with slotted spoon; place on plate, reserving 1 cup liquid. Discard remaining liquid. Return reserved liquid cranberry sauce, chili sauce and chipotle peppers to slow cooker. Stir to combine. Shred pork; stir shredded pork and onion into slow cooker. Cover and cook on LOW for 15 to 20 minutes or until heated through. Divide pork mixture evenly among buns. Makes 12 to 16 sandwiches. (Cooked in a 4-quart slow cooker.)

Helen Joyce M. Alleman
Rayne, La.

Apricot Chicken

4 to 5 lbs. chicken thighs or
    breasts
1 packet onion soup mix

1 bottle Russian dressing
1 jar apricot jam

Mix last 3 ingredients, pour over chicken. Cook for 6 to 8 hours on LOW or 4 to 5 hours on HIGH. Serve over rice.

Chicken Cacciatore #1

1 large onion, sliced thin
1 1/2 lbs. skinless, boneless
   chicken breasts
2 (6-oz.) cans tomato paste
8 oz. fresh sliced mushrooms
1/2 tsp. salt
1/4 tsp. pepper

2 cloves garlic, minced
1 tsp. oregano
1/2 tsp. basil
1 bay leaf
1/4 cup dry white wine
1/4 cup water

Put sliced onion in bottom of slow cooker, and add chicken. Stir together tomato paste, mushrooms, salt, pepper, garlic, herbs, white wine and water. Spread over chicken. Cover and cook on LOW for 7 to 9 hours, or on HIGH for 3 to 4 hours. Serve over hot spaghetti or vermicelli. Makes 4 servings.

Helen Joyce Alleman
Roberts Cove Club, VFC
Rayne, La.

Barbecue Ribs

3 to 4 lbs. spareribs
1/2 tsp. salt
1/2 tsp. pepper

1 large onion, sliced
1 (16-oz.) bottle barbecue sauce

Sprinkle ribs with salt and pepper. Place ribs in a broiler pan under broiler for 15 minutes to brown. Put sliced onion in slow cooker. Slice ribs into serving pieces and put in slow cooker. Pour in barbecue sauce. Cover; cook on LOW 8 to 10 hours, or on HIGH for 4 to 5 hours. Servings 34 – serving size 3 to 4 ribs

Helen Joyce M. Alleman
Roberts Cove Club, VFC
Rayne, La.

Chicken Cacciatore #2

2 medium onions, sliced thin
2 1/2 to 3 lb. broiler, cut in
    pieces
2 cloves garlic, minced
1 lb. whole tomatoes, chopped
1 (8-oz.) can tomato sauce

1 tsp. salt
1/4 tsp. pepper
1 1/2 tsp. oregano
1/2 tsp. basil
1/2 cup chopped celery
1 bay leaf

Place onions in bottom of slow cooker and add chicken. Mix together remaining ingredients and pour over chicken and onions. Cover and cook on LOW for 6 to 8 hours or on HIGH 2 1/2 to 4 hours. Serves six. Cooked in a 3 1/2 quart slow cooker.

Ms. Odile Degeyter
St. Martinville, La.
St. Martin Parish

Barbecue Chicken

Chicken breasts, bone-in   Your favorite barbecue sauce

Put chicken in slow cooker and coat with your favorite barbecue sauce. Cook 4 to 6 hours on LOW or until meat is cooked. Remove chicken from pot and remove meat from bones. Shred the meat, return to sauce in slow cooker and stir together. Serve on buns.

Meat Loaf & Mushrooms

2 slices whole wheat bread
1 lb. ground beef
1 1/2 cups mushrooms, sliced
1/2 cup minced onion
1 tsp. Italian seasoning
3/4 tsp. salt

2 eggs
1 clove garlic, minced
3 tbsp. ketchup
1 1/2 tsp. Dijon mustard
1/8 tsp. ground red pepper

Fold two strips of tin foil, each long enough to fit from the top of the cooker, down inside and up the other side, plus a 2-inch overhang on each side of the cooker – to function as handles for lifting the finished loaf out of the cooker.

Process bread slices in food processor until crumbs measure 1 1/3 cups. Combine bread crumbs, beef, mushrooms, onion, Italian seasoning, salt, eggs and garlic in a bowl. Shape into a loaf; place in slow cooker on top of foil strips. Mix together ketchup, mustard and red pepper. Spread over top of loaf. Cover and cook on LOW 5 hours.

When finished, pull loaf up gently with foil handles. Place loaf on a platter and pull foil handles away. Allow loaf to cool 10 minutes before slicing.

Makes 6 servings. Cooked in a 3 1/2 quart slow cooker.

Elizabeth Lynn, MA
Assistant Extension Agent
Bienville Parish 4-H

Steak Diane

4 beef tenderloins, cut into
   1/4-inch slices
2 tbsp. butter
1 cup mushrooms, sliced
1 tsp. fresh chives, chopped

1 tsp. fresh parsley, minced
1/2 cup beef broth
1 tsp. salt
1/4 tsp. pepper
2 tsp. brandy

Heat the butter in a skillet and sear the steaks for 1 minute. Place the steaks in the slow cooker, then add the mushrooms, chives, parsley, and beef broth. Cook on LOW for 6-8 hours or HIGH for 4-5 hours. During the last 30 minutes of cooking, add the brandy.

Chicken Tortilla Casserole

4 whole boneless chicken breasts, cooked in skillet and cut in 1-in. pieces (reserve 1/4-cup broth chicken was cooked in)

10 (6-in.) flour tortillas, cut in strips about 1/2-in. wide x 2-in. long

2 medium-sized onions, chopped

1 tsp. canola oil

1 (10 3/4-oz.) can fat free chicken broth

1 (10 3/4-oz.) can cream of mushroom soup

2 (4-oz.) cans mild green chilies, chopped

1 egg

1 cup low-fat cheddar cheese, grated

Pour reserved chicken broth in slow cooker sprayed with non-fat cooking spray. Scatter half the tortilla strips in bottom of slow cooker.
Mix remaining ingredients together, except the second half of the tortilla strips and the cheese. Layer half the chicken mixture into the cooker, followed by the other half of the tortillas, followed by the rest of the chicken mix. Cover. Cook on LOW 4-6 hours or on HIGH 3-5 hours. Add the cheese to the top of the dish during the last 20-30 minutes of cooking. Uncover and allow casserole to rest 15 minutes before serving.

Makes 8-10 servings. Cooked in a 5- or 6-quart slow cooker.

Elizabeth Lynn, MA
Assistant Extension Agent
Bienville Parish 4-H

Bratwursts

8 bratwursts
1 large onion, sliced
1 (12-oz.) can beer
1 cup chili sauce
1 tbsp. Worcestershire sauce

1 cup ketchup
2 tbsp. vinegar
1/2 tsp. salt
2 tbsp. brown sugar
1 tbsp. paprika

Boil bratwursts in water in skillet for 10 minutes to remove fat. Drain bratwursts and place in slow cooker. Mix together remaining ingredients in bowl and then pour over meat. Cook on LOW 4-5 hours.
Makes 8 servings. Cooked in a 4-quart slow cooker.

Elizabeth Lynn, MA
Assistant Extension Agent
Bienville Parish 4-H

Chicken in a Pot

2 carrots, sliced
2 onions, sliced
2 celery stalks with leaves cut
    in one-inch pieces
3 lb. broiler or fryer chicken

1 tsp. salt
1/2 tsp. pepper
1/2 cup water, chicken broth or
    white wine
1/2 tsp. basil

Put carrots, onion and celery in bottom of slow cooker. Add whole chicken, and top with salt, pepper and liquid, then sprinkle basil on top. Cover and cook on LOW 8 to 10 hours; (or on HIGH 3 1/2 to 5 hours, using 1 cup water).
Makes 4 servings.

Helen Joyce Alleman
Roberts Cove Club, VFC
Rayne, La.

Chicken Italiano

2 large whole boneless
   chicken breasts, each cut in
   3 pieces
3/4 tsp. salt
1/4 tsp. black pepper
1/4 tsp. dried oregano
1/2 tsp. dried basil
2 bay leaves
1 (26-oz.) jar meatless spaghetti
   sauce

Place chicken in bottom of slow cooker and sprinkle seasonings over chicken. Pour sauce over seasoned meat, stirring to be sure chicken is completely covered. Cover and cook on LOW 6 hours or on HIGH 3 1/2 - 4 hours. Serve over pasta.
Makes 6 servings. Cooked in a 4-quart slow cooker.

Elizabeth Lynn, MA
Assistant Extension Agent
Bienville Parish 4-H

Saucy Apricot Chicken

6 boneless, skinless chicken
   breast halves
2 (12-oz.) jars apricot preserves
1 package dry onion soup mix

Place chicken in slow cooker. Combine apricot preserves and onion soup mix in a separate bowl. Spoon over chicken; cover. Cook on LOW 4-5 hours. Serve with rice. (Cooked in a 6 quart slow cooker.)

Jamie Howell
Bossier City, La.

Corned Beef & Cabbage

3 carrots, cut in 3-inch pieces
3 to 4 lb. corned beef brisket
2 medium onions, quartered

1 cup water
1/2 small head cabbage, cut in
    wedges

Put all ingredients except cabbage wedges in slow cooker in order listed. Cover and cook on LOW 8 to 10 hours, (or HIGH for 5 to 6 hours.) Put cabbage wedges in pot, pushing down to moisten. Cook on HIGH for an additional 2 to 3 hours.
Cabbage: To prepare more cabbage than slow cooker will hold with a large brisket, cook it separately in a skillet. Remove one cup of broth from slow cooker during last hour of cooking. Pour over cabbage wedges in skillet. Cover and cook on LOW heat for 20 to 30 minutes.
Makes 12 to 14 servings.

Helen Joyce Alleman
Roberts Cove Club, VFC
Rayne, La.

Awesome Beef Roast

Small boneless chuck roast
Chopped garlic
1 (24- or 32-oz.) jar Greek salad peppers (pepperoncini)

Stuff roast with chopped garlic. Place the roast into slow cooker. Dump entire jar of peppers and liquid over it. Cook 12 hours on LOW. Stuff the beef, peppers and chopped fresh tomatoes into pita breads, or your favorite bread.

Slow Cooker Chicken

1 chicken, washed, cut up and
    patted dry
2 tbsp. butter, melted
Salt and pepper, to taste
2 tbsp. dry Italian salad dressing mix

1 can mushroom soup
2 (3-oz.) packages cream
    cheese
1/2 cup sherry or water
1 tbsp. chopped onion

Brush chicken with butter. Sprinkle with salt and pepper. Place in slow cooker and sprinkle with dry salad mix. Cook on LOW for 5-6 hours. About 45 minutes before serving mix soup, cream cheese, wine and onion in a small saucepan and cook until smooth. Pour over chicken and cook for 30 minutes on high. Serve over rice. Serves 4 to 6. (Cooked in a 4 quart slow cooker.)

Nancy Unsworth
Doyline, La.

Chicken Curry

28 oz. can diced tomatoes
4 whole boneless, skinless
    chicken breasts, cut into bite
    sized pieces
1 onion, chopped
1/2 green pepper, chopped
1 can cream of celery soup,
    undiluted

2 tbsp. curry powder
1 tsp. turmeric
1/2 tsp. salt
1/4 tsp. pepper
1 tbsp. sugar
1 chicken bouillon cube dissolved in
    1/4 cup hot water

Combine all ingredients in a 6-quart slow cooker, cover and cook on HIGH 2-3 hours or on LOW 5 hours.

Jamie Howell
Bossier City, La.

Pot Roasted Pork

4 to 5 lb. loin end pork roast
1/2 tsp. salt
1/2 tsp. pepper
1 clove garlic, slivered
2 medium onions, sliced

2 bay leaves
1 whole clove
1/2 cup water
1 tbsp. soy sauce

Rub pork roast with salt and pepper. Make tiny slits in meat & insert slivers of garlic. Place roast in broiler pan; broil 15 to 20 minutes to remove excess fat. Put 1 sliced onion in bottom of slow cooker. Add browned pork roast and remaining onion and other ingredients; cover and cook on LOW 10 hours, or HIGH 5 to 6 hours.

Helen Joyce M. Alleman
Rayne, La.

Beef Brisket

1 cup ketchup
1/4 cup grape jelly
1 package dry onion soup

1/2 tsp. black pepper
1 (3 to 3 1/2-lb.) fresh beef brisket, cut in half

Combine ketchup, jelly, onion soup, and pepper and mix well.
Place half of the beef in slow cooker and cover with half of sauce.
Add remaining beef and cover with remaining sauce.
Cover and cook on LOW for 8 to 10 hours or until meat is tender.
Slice and serve with sauce.
– Mrs. Ola Devilbiss
Contributed by Dorothy McCarty

Roast Beef Sandwiches

2 lb. beef top round roast, trimmed
1 can beef broth
1 2/3 cups water
1/2 cup light soy sauce
1 tsp. dried rosemary
1 tsp. dried thyme
1 tsp. garlic powder
1 bay leaf
3 whole peppercorns

Place roast in slow cooker. Add broth, water, soy sauce, and seasonings. Cover and cook on HIGH 5-6 hours. Remove meat from broth and slice thin or shred. Keep warm. Strain broth and skim off fat. Pour broth into small cups for dipping. Serve beef on rolls.

Makes 12 servings. Cooked in a 4-quart slow cooker.

Elizabeth Lynn, MA
Assistant Extension Agent
Bienville Parish 4-H

Beef Roast

1 (2 to 3-lb.) beef roast, cut in half
5 medium potatoes, cut in cubes
1/2 (1-lb.) bag frozen baby carrots
2 cups cherry tomatoes
1/2 cup chopped celery
1/2 cup chopped bell pepper
1 onion, chopped
Dash Worcestershire sauce
1 tbsp. mustard
Salt and pepper, to taste
1 tbsp. parsley flakes

Put all ingredients in slow cooker and top with seasonings. Cook on LOW heat for 8 to 10 hours or until meat is tender. Serve over rice.
– Trisha Ardoin

Easy Slow Cooker Beef

2 to 3 pounds beef chuck, shoulder or blade
1 cup apricot nectar

1/4 cup soy sauce
1 tsp. black pepper
1 medium onion, sliced

Trim visible fat from beef, and discard, cutting the meat into large pieces as you do. Combine beef, nectar, soy sauce, black pepper and onion in slow cooker.
Turn heat to LOW, cover and cook 8 hours or more, until tender.

If you would like to thicken the sauce for gravy, remove the meat and pour the sauce into a shallow saucepan. Let boil until it thickens to desired consistency, about 20 minutes. Serve with sweet potatoes and kale. The sauce tastes good poured over all of them. (Cooked in a 3 1/2 quart slow cooker.)

Serves 6 and leftovers freeze well.

Lois Pryor
Farmerville, La.

Beef Tips

2 lbs. beef tips or stew meat
1 1/2 cans water

1 can cream of mushroom soup
1 envelope dry onion soup mix

Place stew meat in 4 quart slow cooker. Pour water, mushroom soup and dry onion soup mix over meat.
Cook all day in slow cooker on low. Serve over rice.

Connie Aclin, LSU AgCenter
Shreveport, La.

Southwestern Chicken

2 (15 1/4-oz.) cans corn, drained
1 (15-oz.) can black beans, rinsed and drained
1 (10-oz.) jar chunky salsa, divided
6 boneless, skinless chicken breast halves
1 cup shredded cheddar cheese

Combine corn, black beans, and 1/2 cup salsa in slow cooker.
Top with chicken. Pour remaining salsa over chicken.
Cover. Cook on HIGH 3-4 hours or LOW 7-8 hours.
Sprinkle with cheese. Cover 5 minutes for cheese to melt.

Makes 6 servings. Cooked in a 6-quart slow cooker.

Elizabeth Lynn, MA
Assistant Extension Agent
Bienville Parish 4-H

Sour Cream Salsa Chicken

4 skinless, boneless chicken breast halves
1 package taco seasoning mix
1 cup salsa
2 tbsp. cornstarch
1/4 cup sour cream

Place chicken breasts in slow cooker. Sprinkle with taco seasoning. Top with salsa. Cook on LOW for 6 to 8 hours.
Before serving, remove the chicken from the pot. Combine 2 tbsp. corn starch in a small amount of cold water. Stir well. Stir the cornstarch mixture into salsa sauce in slow cooker. Stir in 1/4 cup of sour cream. Cook for 30 minutes on HIGH or until mixture has thickened. Makes 4 servings. (Cooked in a 6 quart slow cooker.)

Nicole Aclin
Little Rock, Ark.

Chuck Roast Barbecue

2 1/2 lb. boneless chuck roast, trimmed
2 medium onions, chopped
1 (12-oz.) can cola
1/3 cup Worcestershire sauce
1 1/2 tbsp. apple cider vinegar or white vinegar
1 1/2 tsp. beef bouillon granules
3/4 tsp. dry mustard
3/4 tsp. chili powder
1/4 to 1/2 tsp. ground red pepper
1 cup ketchup
1 tbsp. butter or margarine
6 hamburger buns

Place roast in a 4 quart electric slow cooker; add onions. To make a sauce, combine cola, Worcestershire sauce, vinegar, beef bouillon, dry mustard, chili powder and red pepper in a bowl; cover. Reserve 1 cup of the sauce and chill. Pour remaining sauce over roast. Cover and cook on HIGH 6 hours or LOW 9 hours or until roast is very tender. Remove roast with chopped onion from cooker, using a slotted spoon, and shred meat with two forks. (Reserve remaining meat juices to spoon over mashed potatoes or toast, if desired.)

Combine reserved sauce, ketchup, and butter in a saucepan; cook over medium heat, stirring constantly, until thoroughly heated. Pour sauce over shredded meat, stirring gently. Spoon meat mixture onto buns. Yield: 6 servings

Casey Davis
Bossier City, La.

Creole Steak

1 1/2 lb. boneless round steak
Salt and pepper, to taste
1/4 tsp. garlic powder
1 onion, chopped
1 cup sliced celery
1 cup seasoned tomato juice

2 tsp. Worcestershire sauce
1 medium green bell pepper,
   chopped
1 (10-oz.) package frozen
   okra (or 1 1/2 cups fresh)
2 1/2 oz. sliced mushrooms

Cut steak into strips, about 2 inches long and 1/2 inch wide. Season with salt, pepper and garlic powder. Place in slow cooker with onion, celery, tomato juice, and Worcestershire sauce. Cover and cook on LOW for 6 to 8 hours.
Turn setting to HIGH. Add bell pepper and partially thawed okra and mushrooms. Cover and cook for 30 minutes until okra is done.

Chicken Tacos

1 lb. boneless, skinless chicken breasts
1 packet taco seasoning

1 cup chicken broth

Combine in slow cooker; cook 6 to 8 hours on LOW. Remove breasts and fork-shred. Spoon a bit of the juice over it if desired. Serve on warmed tacos or tortillas with cheese, salsa, sour cream, black olives.
This freezes very well.

Pork Roast

2 lb. Boston butt roast
Salt and pepper, to taste
5 cloves garlic
2-3 tbsp. cooking oil

1 medium onion
2 cups cubed potatoes
1 cup thick sliced potatoes
1 cup sliced mushrooms

Salt and pepper all sides of the roast. Make holes in the roast with sharp knife; insert garlic cloves into holes. Brown roast in cooking oil using an iron skillet. Place roast in slow cooker.

Add 1 cup hot water to iron skillet before adding mixture to slow cooker. Slice onion and place on top of meat. Cook on HIGH for 1 hour then reduce temperature to LOW for 3 hours. After 3 hours place potatoes, carrots and mushrooms around roast and continue to cook on LOW temperature overnight.
Cooked in a 2-quart slow cooker.

Glynda Brown
Shreveport, La.

Pork Chops in Chicken Rice Soup

6 pork chops
Salt and pepper, to taste

26-oz. can chicken rice soup

Brown pork chops well and season lightly with salt and pepper. Place in slow cooker and cover with soup. Cover and cook on HIGH 3 hours or LOW on 5-7 hours. (Cooked in a 5-quart slow cooker).

Barbara Coe
Minden, La.

Super Easy Pork Chops

4 pork chops, about an inch
thick
Cajun seasoning, to taste
Salt and pepper, to taste
2 tsp. cooking oil
1 clove garlic, minced

3 tbsp. soy sauce
1/4 cup chicken broth
2 tbsp. brown sugar or honey
Dash cayenne pepper
1 tsp. corn starch mixed with 1 tbsp.
water to make smooth paste

Season pork chops with Cajun seasoning, salt, & pepper to taste. In a skillet over medium heat, warm cooking oil. Add pork chops and sear until browned on both sides. Transfer pork chops to slow cooker. Add garlic to pan drippings and sauté until it beings to brown; stir in soy sauce, broth, sugar, and cayenne pepper. Stir to blend, bring just to a boil. Pour sauce over chops. Cover and cook on LOW until pork chops are tender, about 6 to 7 hours. Stir in cornstarch and water mixture until well blended. Cover and cook about 20 minutes longer.
(Cooked in a 4-quart slow cooker.)

Laura Martin Haley
Doyline, La.

Barbecued Pork on Buns

2 lbs. boneless pork loin
1 onion, chopped
3/4 cup cola carbonated beverage

3/4 cup barbecue sauce
8 sandwich buns

Combine all ingredients except buns in slow cooker. Cook, covered on HIGH for 5 to 6 hours or until very tender. Drain and slice or shred pork; serve on buns with additional barbecue sauce, if desired. Makes 8 servings. Cooked in a 4-quart slow cooker.

NOTE: Pork can be made 1 to 2 days ahead; cover and refrigerate. Reheat before serving.

Cajun Pepper Steak

To be served over hot rice, a baked potato or pasta.

1 to 2 lbs. boneless round
    steak, cut into bite-size
    pieces or thin strips, then
    seasoned thoroughly with
    Cajun seasoning
1 (10.5-oz.) can beef broth
1 (10-oz.) can diced tomatoes
    with green chilies
1/2 large onion, chopped

1/2 bell pepper, chopped
5 garlic cloves, minced
2 tsp. Worcestershire sauce
1/8 tsp. dried bay leaf flakes
1/2 tsp. dried basil
TABASCO® Brand Pepper Sauce to
    taste, or serve at the table
1 (.87-oz.) envelope Brown Gravy
    Mix

Add all ingredients to slow cooker. Empty gravy mix into 1 cup of hot water, stir to dissolve, and add to slow cooker. Cook on HIGH for 3 hours, or on LOW for 6 hours.
Makes 1 1/2 quarts.

Neal Bertrand
Lafayette, La.

Baby Back Ribs

1 rack baby back ribs
2 tbsp. Cajun seasoning

1/2 cup water
12 oz. of your favorite barbecue sauce

Cut rack into sections of 3 ribs each. Season, add water and cook in slow cooker on LOW for 7 hours. Remove ribs, drain out juice, place ribs back in slow cooker, add barbecue sauce and cook on LOW for one hour.

Cliff & Amy Amox
Arnaudville, La.

Easy Smothered Potatoes & Sausage

This savory meal goes well as a side or main dish.

3 links (1 lb.) smoked sausage, cut in small pieces
1 (2-lb.) bag frozen, crinkle-cut French-fried potatoes, defrosted

1 (1-oz.) package onion soup mix, dissolved in 3/4 cup water
1 onion, chopped
4 cloves garlic, minced
Salt, red & black pepper, to taste
1/2 stick butter, chopped

Brown sausage in skillet, drain excess grease.
Add all ingredients to slow cooker, stir, cover and cook on HIGH for 3 1/2 hours, or on LOW for 6 or 7 hours.

Makes two quarts.

Neal Bertrand
Lafayette, La.

Cheap Cola Roast

1 roast
1 envelope dry onion soup mix
12 ounces cola, (not diet)

Place the roast in the slow cooker. Sprinkle onion soup mix over it and add cola. Cook on LOW all day long. Leave it in for 12 hours if you like it to fall apart.

Orange-Glazed Chicken Breast

1 (6-oz.) can frozen orange
 juice concentrate, undiluted
1/2 tsp. dried marjoram leaves

6 (6-oz.) chicken breast halves, skin
 and excess fat removed
1/4 cup water
2 tbsp. cornstarch

Combine thawed orange juice and marjoram in shallow dish. Dip each breast in orange juice mixture and put in slow cooker. Pour remaining sauce over breasts. Cover and cook on LOW for 7 to 9 hours; or cook on HIGH for 4 to 5 hours. To thicken sauce, add water and cornstarch, and stir well.
Makes 6 servings.

Helen Joyce Alleman
Roberts Cove Club, VFC
Rayne, La.

Fall-Off-The-Bone Barbecue Ribs

1 medium onion, chopped
1/2 cup ketchup
1/4 cup cider vinegar
1/4 cup packed brown sugar
1/4 cup tomato paste

2 tbsp. paprika or smoked paprika
2 tbsp. Worcestershire sauce
1 tbsp. yellow mustard
1 tsp. salt
1 tsp. black pepper
4 lbs. pork spareribs

In a 4 1/2 or 6 quart slow cooker bowl, stir-in all ingredients except ribs, until combined. Add ribs, cutting into several large pieces to fit in slow cooker bowl. Spoon sauce over and around ribs to coat. Cover and cook on LOW 8 to 10 hours or on HIGH for 4 to 5 hours. Transfer ribs to platter. Skim and discard fat from cooking liquid. Spoon remaining liquid over ribs.

Mexican Corn Bread

1 lb. ground beef or venison
1 (10-oz.) can cream-style corn
1 cup cornmeal
1/2 tsp. baking soda
1 tsp. salt
1/4 cup oil
1 cup milk

2 eggs, beaten
1/2 cup taco sauce
2 cups shredded cheddar cheese
1 medium sized onion, chopped
1 garlic clove, minced
1 (4-oz.) can diced green chilies

Brown meat in skillet.

While meat is browning, combine corn, cornmeal, baking soda, salt, oil, milk, eggs and taco sauce in a bowl. Pour half of mixture into slow cooker.

Layer cheese, onion, garlic, green chilies, and ground beef on top of cornmeal mixture; cover with remaining cornmeal mixture. Cover and cook on HIGH 1 hour then on LOW 3 1/2 - 4 hours; or only on LOW 6 hours.

Makes 6 servings. Cooked in a 4-quart slow cooker.

Elizabeth Lynn, MA
Assistant Extension Agent, LSU AgCenter
Bienville Parish 4-H

Pork Chops

1/4 cup olive oil
1 cup chicken broth
2 cloves garlic, minced
1 tbsp. paprika
1 tbsp. garlic powder

1 tbsp. poultry seasoning
1 tsp. dried oregano
1 tsp. dried basil
4 thick-cut boneless pork chops
Salt and pepper, to taste

In a large bowl, whisk together the olive oil, chicken broth, garlic, paprika, garlic powder, poultry seasoning, oregano and basil. Pour into the slow cooker. Cut small slits in each pork chop with the tip of a knife, and season lightly with salt and pepper. Place pork chops into the slow cooker, cover, and cook on HIGH for 4 hours or on LOW for 7 or 8 hours. Baste periodically with the sauce.

Sausage Sauce Piquante

Here's a basic sauce piquante (pronounced pee-KAHNT) dish that I made with sausage. It can be made with any kind of meat or seafood. It is usually eaten over hot, fluffy rice, but this is another dish that would taste great mixed in with baked potatoes.

1 lb. sausage of your choice, cut in small pieces
1 (6-oz.) can tomato paste
1 (8-oz.) can tomato sauce
1 (10-oz.) can diced tomatoes with green chilies
1 large onion, chopped
4 cloves garlic, minced
1 bell pepper, chopped (or 1/2 green and 1/2 red bell pepper)
1/2 cup chopped green onion
Parsley, to taste
Salt and pepper, to taste
1 tsp. sugar to cut acidity of tomato sauce
1 cup water
Hot rice or potatoes

Add all ingredients to slow cooker except rice; stir, cover and cook on HIGH for 3 hours, or on LOW for 6 hours.
Serve over hot rice or baked or mashed potatoes.
Makes about one quart.

Neal Bertrand
Lafayette, La.

Sweet & Sour Hamburger

1 to 2 lbs. ground beef or turkey, browned
1 can cranberry sauce
1 can diced tomatoes or tomato sauce

Add all ingredients to slow cooker. Cover and cook on LOW for 6 hours or so. Serve with rice or noodles.

PASTAS

Chicken Breast & Turkey Sausage Pastalaya

You've heard of jambalaya, right? This is the simplest version of traditional jambalaya, but with a twist... pasta instead of rice! Hence the name...Pastalaya.

1 (10.5-oz.) can beef broth
1/2 cup water
1/2 lb. chicken breast, sliced into bite-size pieces
1/2 lb. (1 1/2 links) turkey sausage, sliced into small pieces
Cajun or Creole seasoning, to taste

TABASCO® Brand Pepper Sauce to taste, or serve at the table
1/2 stick butter, chopped
1 (10-oz.) can diced tomatoes with green chilies
1 onion, chopped fine
1/2 bell pepper, chopped fine
5 cloves garlic, minced
8-oz. pack elbow macaroni, cooked according to package directions

Coat the chicken and sausage with Cajun seasoning; brown for 10 minutes in skillet.
Add all ingredients except pasta to slow cooker, stir, cover and cook on LOW for 7 hours. Add cooked macaroni to slow cooker, being careful not to add too much and overcrowd it, stir well, and serve.
Makes 1 3/4 quarts.

Neal Bertrand
Lafayette, La.

Spaghetti & Meatballs

A traditional family favorite made easy. For convenience, buy the two-pound bag of 32 flame broiled, Italian Style meatballs found in the frozen foods section of the supermarket. They work great. This classic Italian dish is super easy and super tasty!

12 frozen cooked meatballs
1 (16-oz.) jar spaghetti sauce

1 onion, chopped
3 cloves garlic, minced

1/2 cup chopped green onion

1/2 cup chopped parsley

Salt, black & red pepper, to taste

1 tsp. oregano

1 (7-oz.) box spaghetti

Add all ingredients to slow cooker except spaghetti. Cook on LOW for 3 hours. Cook spaghetti on stove according to package directions, then add to slow cooker and mix well.

Serve hot with your favorite cheese.

Makes 2 quarts.

Neal Bertrand
Lafayette, La.

Chicken & Cheesy Macaroni

"Kids" of all ages will love this one.

1 1/2 lbs. chicken breast, or your favorite parts, cut into bite-size pieces

Salt and pepper, to taste

1/2 large bell pepper, chopped

1 small onion, chopped

1 (10.5-oz.) can cream of celery soup

1 (10.5-oz.) can chicken broth

1 (8-oz.) package of your favorite shredded cheese

2 cups elbow macaroni

Brown chicken in skillet and season well; add all ingredients (except cheese and macaroni) to slow cooker, stir, cover and cook on LOW for two hours.

Cook macaroni on stove according to package directions.

Then add macaroni and cheese to slow cooker, stir well until cheese is melted and serve immediately.

Makes 1 3/4 quarts.

Neal Bertrand
Lafayette, La.

Tex-Mex Pasta

Pasta with a Tex-Mex twist!

**1 lb. ground beef or turkey,
    browned**
**Salt, red and black pepper, to
    taste**
**1 (10-oz.) can diced tomatoes
    with green chilies**
1 (8-oz.) can tomato sauce
1 (10.5-oz.) can beef broth

1 tsp. onion powder
1 tsp. garlic powder
2 tsp. chili powder
Pinch of cumin, optional
**TABASCO® Brand Pepper Sauce to
    taste, or serve at the table**
**1 (12-oz.) package of your favorite
    pasta**

Brown meat in skillet, drain excess liquid, and season with salt and
pepper. Add all ingredients to slow cooker except pasta, stir, cover and
cook on LOW for three hours.
Cook pasta on stove according to package directions, then add cooked
pasta to slow cooker and stir well to blend together.
Serve immediately.

Makes 2 quarts.

Neal Bertrand
Lafayette, La.

Cheesy Noodle Goulash

What a cheesy treat!

*NOTE: We recommend cooking pasta on the stove according to your
taste, and adding the cooked pasta to the slow cooker when meal is
ready. Cooking the pasta in the slow cooker can result in a great meal,
but can also be overcooked and mushy.*

1 lb. ground beef, browned
Salt & pepper, to taste
1 tsp. chili powder
1 (8-oz.) can tomato sauce
1 (10-oz.) can diced tomatoes
  with green chilies
1 onion, chopped

3 garlic cloves, minced
TABASCO® Brand Pepper Sauce to
  taste, or serve at the table
2 cups egg noodles, uncooked
1/4-lb. block of processed cheese cut
  in pieces

Brown the meat in skillet, drain excess liquid, then season the meat with salt, pepper and chili powder.

Add all ingredients to slow cooker except noodles and cheese, stir, cover and cook on LOW for 2 1/4 hours. Cook noodles on stove according to package directions.
Add noodles and cheese, stir well to mix, and then serve.

Makes 1 1/4 quarts.

Neal Bertrand
Lafayette, La.

Macaroni & Cheese

2 cups dry macaroni noodles
1 stick margarine
2 lb. box Velveeta cheese, diced

3 cups milk
1/4 tsp. Creole seasoning

Cook macaroni on stove until almost tender. In a slow cooker on HIGH, mix margarine and cheese until melted. Add semi cooked macaroni, milk, and seasoning and stir well. Set slow cooker on LOW, and cook for 30 minutes, stirring occasionally. (Cooked in a 6-quart slow cooker.)

Emily Aclin
Shreveport, La.

Hearty Corn & Black-Eyed Pea Pastalaya

1 lb. ground beef, browned in skillet, drained

Salt, black and red pepper, to taste

1 (15.25-oz.) can whole kernel corn, undrained

1 (15.5-oz.) can black-eyed peas, undrained

1 (10-oz.) can diced tomatoes with green chilies

1 (10.5-oz.) can beef broth

1 (10.5-oz.) can cream of celery soup

1/2 bell pepper, chopped

1 onion, chopped

3 cloves garlic, minced

1 tsp. onion powder

1 tsp. garlic powder

TABASCO® Brand Pepper Sauce to taste, or serve at the table

2 cups elbow macaroni, cooked according to package directions.

Season browned beef with salt and peppers; place in slow cooker. Add all remaining ingredients to slow cooker except pasta, stir, cover and cook on HIGH for 3 hours, or on LOW for 6 hours. Add cooked pasta to slow cooker, mix together and serve immediately.

Makes 2 1/2 quarts.

Neal Bertrand
Lafayette, La.

Chicken & Pasta

A savory and quick meal!

1 lb. chicken breast, or your favorite chicken parts, cut in bite-size pieces

Salt and pepper, to taste

1 (10-oz.) can diced tomatoes with green chilies

1 (8-oz.) can tomato sauce

1/2 stick butter, chopped

1/2 large bell pepper, chopped

1 onion, chopped

3 cloves garlic, chopped

2 cups large elbow macaroni, cooked according to package directions

1/4 lb. block of processed cheese cut in pieces

Season chicken pieces well and brown in skillet. Add browned chicken and all remaining ingredients, except pasta and cheese, to slow cooker, stir, cover and cook on LOW for 3 or 4 hours. Add pasta and cheese, stir well to mix, and then serve.

Makes about 2 quarts.

Neal Bertrand
Lafayette, La.

Crawfish or Shrimp Fettuccine

A classic Cajun dish that can easily be done in your slow cooker.
Note: The diced tomatoes with green chilies and the cheese dip both have a little pepper flavor, so go easy on adding extra pepper. Shrimp may be substituted if crawfish are not available.

1 (10-oz.) can diced tomatoes with green chilies
1 (10.5-oz.) can chicken broth
1/2 stick butter, chopped
1 onion, chopped fine
1/2 large bell pepper, chopped fine
4 cloves garlic, minced
1/2 cup chopped green onion
1/2 tsp. dried parsley
1/4 tsp. Cajun or Creole seasoning
1 lb. peeled crawfish tails
1 (15-oz.) jar salsa con queso cheese dip, "medium" flavor
1 (12-oz. box) fettuccine noodles

Add all ingredients to slow cooker, except seafood, cheese dip and noodles. Stir well, cover and cook for 2 1/2 hours on high. Add seafood one hour before ready to serve. Cook on LOW for one hour.
Cook fettuccine according to package directions, and then add to slow cooker along with cheese dip and stir well to mix.
Serve hot.

Makes 2 1/4 quarts.

Neal Bertrand
Lafayette, La.

Pizza Pastalaya

No need to call the pizza man tonight! This one will get your family's attention.

1 lb. lean ground beef or turkey, browned, drained
Salt and pepper, to taste
1 (10-oz.) can beef broth
1 (1 lb. 10-oz.) jar spaghetti or pizza sauce
4 oz. pepperoni slices
1 medium onion, chopped
3 cloves garlic, minced
1 small bell pepper, chopped
TABASCO® Brand Pepper Sauce to taste, or serve at the table
Shredded Mozzarella cheese
2 cups elbow macaroni, uncooked

In a skillet, brown the meat and season well with salt and pepper.
Add all remaining ingredients to slow cooker except cheese and macaroni, stir, cover and cook on LOW for 3 1/2 hours.
Cook the macaroni in a pot on stove according to package directions.
Add cooked macaroni to slow cooker, stir well to combine and serve; add cheese on top of each serving.

Makes 2 1/4 quarts.

Neal Bertrand
Lafayette, La.

SEAFOOD

Crawfish & Corn Maque Choux

Corn Maque Choux (pronounced mock-shoe) is a traditional dish of southern Louisiana. We're adding crawfish to make an excellent meal everyone is sure to love. Also try our Crawfish & Corn Maque Choux Soup in the Soups chapter.

1 (14.75-oz.) can sweet cream corn
1 (15.25-oz.) can whole kernel sweet corn, drained
1 (10-oz.) can diced tomatoes with green chilies
1 onion, chopped
1 bell pepper, chopped
1 stalk celery, chopped
4 cloves garlic, minced
1 stick butter, chopped
Salt, red and black pepper, to taste
1 lb. crawfish tails, peeled and deveined
Hot cooked rice

Add all ingredients to slow cooker except crawfish and rice, stir well, cover and cook on LOW for 6 or 7 hours or on HIGH for 3 or 4 hours, or until vegetables are tender. Add crawfish and cook on LOW for 1 hour. Serve over hot rice.

Makes 2 quarts.

Neal Bertrand
Lafayette, La.

Cajun Shrimp Creole

1 tbsp. butter
2 cups onion, chopped
2 tbsp. buttermilk biscuit mix
1 1/2 cups water
1 (6-oz.) can tomato paste
1 tsp. salt
1/4 tsp. sugar
1 bay leaf
1/8 cup jalapeno pepper
1/2 cup celery, chopped
1/2 cup green pepper, chopped
2 lbs. frozen shrimp, thawed, shelled & cleaned

In a skillet, melt the butter, add the onion, and cook slightly. Add the biscuit mix and stir until well blended. Combine remaining ingredients except shrimp and add to slow cooker along with onion mixture. Cook on LOW for 7 to 9 hours. Add the shrimp during the last hour of cooking.

Contributed by Mimi Stoker

Crawfish Étouffée

Here's a classic all-time favorite of south Louisiana's Cajun Country. Crawfish étouffée (pronounced A-two-FAY) is a real treat when traveling down here and visiting our popular restaurants. Now you can enjoy it from the comfort of your home.
Note: Shrimp may be substituted for crawfish.

1/2 stick butter, chopped
1/2 small red bell pepper, chopped
1/2 small green bell pepper, chopped
3 green onions, chopped
3 cloves garlic, minced
1 medium onion, chopped
1/4 cup minced parsley
2 dashes (1/8 tsp.) dried bay leaf flakes

1 tbsp. Worcestershire sauce
1 (10.5-oz.) cans chicken broth
1 (10.5-oz.) can cream of mushroom or cream of celery soup
Salt and pepper, to taste
TABASCO® Brand Pepper Sauce to taste, or serve at the table
2 tbsp. flour
1 lb. crawfish tails, peeled and deveined
Hot cooked rice

Add all ingredients to slow cooker except flour, crawfish and rice. Stir to blend well, then stir in the flour a little at a time, stirring constantly, so it blends thoroughly.
Cook on HIGH for 3 hours. One hour before ready to eat, add crawfish and cook on LOW for one hour. Serve over hot rice.
Makes about one quart.

Neal Bertrand
Lafayette, La.

Crawfish Stew

I grew up eating Mom's stews and gumbos cooked with roux (pronounced roo).
It has a brown color and an excellent taste. Roux can be made on the stove with equal parts oil and all-purpose flour, but I cheat and go the easy route and use a store-bought roux that I have good success with.

Shrimp, fish or chicken cut in bite-size pieces may be substituted in place of crawfish.

1 lb. peeled crawfish tails
1 tsp. Cajun or Creole seasoning
1/2 stick butter, chopped
1 onion, chopped
1/2 bell pepper, chopped
2 cloves garlic, minced
2 green onions, chopped
1 tbsp. Worcestershire sauce

TABASCO® Brand Pepper Sauce to taste, or serve at the table
1/4 cup Tony Chachere's Roux Mix dissolved in 2 cups water in a pot on stove
1 extra cup water
Hot cooked rice

Put the crawfish tails in a bowl, season well, cover and then reserve in refrigerator. Add next seven ingredients.

To make the roux, add two cups cool water to a saucepan, slowly stir in the roux mix and dissolve well. Place on the stove and heat to help completely dissolve roux. Pour the heated roux/water mixture into slow cooker, add one extra cup of water, stir well, cover and cook on LOW for 6 to 7 hours. One hour before ready to eat, add crawfish and cook on LOW for 1 hour or until crawfish are cooked.

Serve over hot cooked rice.

Makes almost 2 quarts.

Salmon with Caramelized Onions & Carrots

1 (8-oz.) bag baby carrots
1 (10-oz.) bag pearl onions, peeled
2 tbsp. olive oil
2 tbsp. butter
1 tsp. brown sugar

1 tbsp. minced garlic
1/4 tsp. dill
1/8 tsp. rosemary
1/2 tsp. Cajun seasoning
1 1/2 lbs. fresh salmon fillet

Add carrots, onions, olive oil, butter, brown sugar, and minced garlic into slow cooker and cook on LOW for 7-8 hours. Season salmon with dill, rosemary, and Cajun seasoning.
Add salmon to slow cooker and cook on LOW for 1 1/2 - 2 hours, or until done.

Cliff & Amy Amox
Arnaudville, La.

Crawfish Jambalaya Stew

If crawfish are not available, use shrimp.

1 (10.5-oz.) can chicken broth
1 (8-oz.) can tomato sauce
1 (4-oz.) can mushroom pieces, optional
1 jalapeno pepper, finely chopped
1 medium yellow onion, chopped

1/2 medium bell pepper, chopped
1/2 stick butter, chopped
TABASCO® Brand Pepper Sauce to taste, or serve at the table
1 lb. peeled crawfish tails seasoned with Cajun or Creole seasoning, to taste
Hot, fluffy rice

Put all ingredients in a slow cooker except crawfish and rice. Cook on HIGH for 5 hours. Then add crawfish and cook on LOW for 1 hour longer. Serve over hot rice.
Makes almost 2 quarts.

Neal Bertrand
Lafayette, La.

Shrimp Creole Jambalaya Stew

I call this a stew because it is served over hot cooked rice. But I have also cooked it in my rice cooker along with rice and it made a great jambalaya.

1 lb. shrimp, peeled and deveined
2 tsp. Cajun or Creole seasoning, or to taste
1 (10-oz.) can diced tomatoes with green chilies, with liquid
2 tbsp. tomato paste
1/2 stick butter, chopped
1/2 cup chopped green onion

1/2 green bell pepper, chopped
1/2 red bell pepper, chopped
2 stalks celery, chopped
4 cloves garlic, minced
1 cup water
1/2 cup chopped mushrooms, optional
2 tbsp. Worcestershire sauce
1 tsp. salt

Season the shrimp thoroughly with seasoning, then cover and set aside in refrigerator.
Add remaining ingredients to slow cooker, and cook on LOW for 7 hours; then add shrimp and cook for one hour on LOW or until pink.
Serve over hot rice.

Neal Bertrand
Lafayette, La.

"This was an absolutely delicious dish. It would make a good company meal with a salad or cole slaw and dessert. I love this dish. It's a keeper."

Trish Gregory, Florida

Catfish Sauce Piquante

Catfish cooked in tomato gravy is a Cajun/Creole classic dish. You may substitute the catfish for the fish of your choice.

1 lb. catfish fillets, cut into bite-size pieces
2 tsp. or more Cajun or Creole seasoning, to taste
TABASCO® Brand Pepper Sauce to taste, or serve at the table
1 (10-oz.) can diced tomatoes with green chilies
1 (6-oz.) can tomato paste
1 onion, chopped
1 medium bell pepper, chopped
7 cloves garlic, minced
3 green onion tops, chopped
1/2 stick butter, chopped
1/2 tsp. sugar
1 cup water
Hot, fluffy rice

Put the catfish pieces in a bowl and season well; cover and reserve in refrigerator. Add remaining ingredients to slow cooker except rice. Stir, cover and cook on LOW for 7 hours, then add catfish and cook for 1 hour on LOW or until fish is cooked.
Serve over hot rice.

Makes 2 1/2 quarts.

Neal Bertrand
Lafayette, La.

"I made this dish tonight and it was delicious. I would definitely make it again. My husband loves it and says that it's a keeper. It would be good with chicken or shrimp, too. For vegetarians it could be used alone over rice or pasta. I have given the recipe to 3 other friends."
Trish Gregory, Florida

Shrimp Creole

1 1/2 cups chopped onion
3/4 cup chopped celery
1 clove garlic, minced
3/4 cup diced green pepper
1 (28-oz.) can whole tomatoes
2 (8-oz.) cans tomato sauce
1/2 tsp. salt
1/2 tsp. pepper

1 tsp. sugar
1 tsp. paprika
1 bay leaf
3 to 6 drops TABASCO® sauce
1 lb. fresh shrimp, shelled and
    deveined; or 1 (16-oz.) package
    frozen shelled shrimp, rinsed and
    drained.

Combine all ingredients except shrimp in slow cooker, and stir to blend well. Cover and cook on LOW 7 to 9 hours, or HIGH for 3 to 4 hours. During the last hour turn to HIGH and add shrimp. Cook one hour or until shrimp turn pink.
Makes six servings.

Helen Joyce Alleman
Roberts Cove Club, VFC
Rayne, La.

Shrimp Marinara

1 (16-oz.) can tomatoes, cut up
2 tbsp. minced parsley
1 clove garlic, minced
1/2 tsp. dried basil
1 tsp. salt
1/4 tsp. pepper

1 tsp. dried oregano
1 (6-oz.) can tomato paste
1/2 tsp. seasoned salt
1 lb. cooked shelled shrimp
Grated Parmesan cheese
Cooked spaghetti

In a slow cooker, combine tomatoes with parsley, garlic, basil, salt, pepper, oregano, tomato paste and seasoned salt. Cover and cook on LOW for 6 to 7 hours. Turn heat to HIGH, stir in shrimp, cover and cook on high for 10 to 15 minutes more. Serve over cooked spaghetti.

SOUPS, STEWS & CHILI

Cream Cheese Potato Soup

3 cups water
1 cup ham, diced
5 medium-sized potatoes, diced fine
1 (8-oz.) package cream cheese, cubed

1/2 med onion, chopped
1 tsp. garlic salt
1/2 tsp. black pepper
1/2 tsp. dill weed

Combine all ingredients in slow cooker. Cover and cook on HIGH 4 hours, stirring occasionally. Turn to LOW until ready to serve.
Makes 6 servings. Cooked in a 3 1/2-quart slow cooker.

Elizabeth Lynn, MA
Assistant Extension Agent
Bienville Parish 4-H

Chicken & White Bean Stew

2 lbs. skinless, boneless chicken
   thighs
2 tsp. ground cumin
1/8 tsp. ground black pepper
1 tbsp. olive oil
2 (10-oz.) packages refrigerated
   light Alfredo sauce
1 (15-oz.) can Great Northern or
   white kidney beans, rinsed
   and drained

1 cup reduced sodium chicken broth
1/2 cup chopped red onion
1 (4-oz.) can diced green chili
   peppers
4 cloves garlic, minced
1/4 cup shredded sharp cheddar
   cheese or Monterey Jack cheese,
   optional

Cut chicken into 1-inch pieces. Sprinkle chicken with cumin and pepper. In a large skillet, cook chicken, half at a time, in hot oil over medium heat until brown. Place chicken in slow cooker. Stir in Alfredo sauce, beans, broth, onion, chili peppers and garlic. Cover and cook on LOW for 4 to 5 hours or on HIGH for 2 to 2 1/2 hours. If desired, sprinkle each serving with cheese and parsley.
Makes 8 servings. Cooked in a 3 1/2 or 4 quart slow cooker.

Janet Lasseigne
Parks, La.

Meatball Mushroom Soup

1/2 lb. ground turkey, beef or venison
1/2 tsp. garlic powder
1/2 tsp. onion powder
1/2 tsp. black pepper
1 large egg
1 tbsp. olive oil
1 cup carrots, thinly sliced
2 cloves garlic, crushed
2 cups fresh mushrooms, sliced
1 (10 3/4-oz.) can beef broth
1 (10 3/4-oz.) can cream of mushroom soup
2 tbsp. tomato paste
Parmesan cheese for garnish
Fresh parsley for garnish

In a small bowl mix together meat and seasonings. Add egg, stirring until well blended. Form into small meatballs. Heat olive oil in skillet. Brown meatballs. Drain well. Transfer meatballs to slow cooker. Add remaining ingredients, except Parmesan cheese and parsley.
Cover and cook on LOW 6-8 hours or on HIGH for 3-4 hours.

Makes 8 Servings. Cooked in a 3 1/2-quart slow cooker.

Elizabeth Lynn, MA
Assistant Extension Agent
Bienville Parish 4-H

Taco Soup #1

1 lb. ground venison
1 small onion, chopped
1 (4-oz.) can chopped green
  chilies, undrained
1/2 tsp. salt
1 package taco seasoning mix
1 package Ranch style dressing
  mix

3 (14 1/2-oz.) cans diced tomatoes,
  undrained (for extra spice use one
  can Rotel tomatoes)
1 (16-oz.) can kidney beans,
  undrained
1 (15-oz.) can pinto beans, undrained
1 1/2 cups water

Mix all ingredients together in large slow cooker, cover, and cook on
LOW 9-10 hours. (Cooked in a 4-quart slow cooker.)

Makes 8 Servings

Elizabeth Lynn, MA
Assistant Extension Agent
Bienville Parish 4-H

Ham & Potato Chowder

5-oz. package scalloped
  potatoes with sauce mix
1 cup cooked ham, cut into
  strips or bite size pieces
4 cups chicken broth

1 cup chopped celery
1/3 cup chopped onion
1/2 tsp. pepper
2 cups half and half
1/3 cup flour

Combine potatoes, sauce mix, ham, broth, celery, onion, and pepper in
slow cooker. Cover. Cook on LOW 7 hours in a 6 quart slow cooker.
Combine half and half and flour. Gradually add to slow cooker, blending
well. Cover. Cook on LOW up to 1 hour, stirring occasionally until
thickened.

Dianne Glasgow
Bossier City, La.

Taco Soup #2

2 lbs. ground meat
1 large onion, chopped
3 (14 1/2-oz.) cans stewed
  tomatoes
1 (15.2-oz.) can whole kernel
  sweet corn with liquid

1 (15-oz.) can pinto beans with liquid
1 (15-oz.) can Texas-style beans
1 envelope Ranch dressing mix
1 (1.5 oz.) envelope taco seasoning
  mix
1 (15-oz.) can chilies (optional)

Brown ground meat and onion together. Remove from heat, drain off liquid, then place in slow cooker with all remaining ingredients.
Put slow cooker on LOW and cook for 8 hours.
When serving, sprinkle soup with grated cheese and serve with crackers of your choice. (Cooked in a 4-quart slow cooker.)

Serves 6 to 8.

Mrs. Nell DuBose
Tickfaw, La.

Navy Bean Soup

1 lb. sausage, browned, and
  drained
1 onion, chopped, sautéed
4 cans navy beans

1 cup chopped ham
1 bay leaf
1 can tomatoes with peppers
Season with pepper

Brown sausage and drain well. Sauté onion until clear. Put all in slow cooker. As you empty beans rinse each can with a little water and add to pot. Put on LOW to cook all day or HIGH for half a day. Good with broccoli cornbread.

Connie Aclin, LSU AgCenter
Shreveport, La.

Taco Soup #3

What great Mexican flavors! Feel free to increase the seasoning level if you wish.

1 lb. ground meat, browned
Salt and pepper, to taste
1/2 tsp. chili powder
1/2 tsp. garlic powder
1/2 tsp. onion powder
1 (15.25-oz.) can whole kernel corn, undrained
1 (15.5-oz.) can chili beans, undrained
1 (10-oz.) can diced tomatoes with green chilies, undrained
1 medium onion, chopped
1 (8-oz.) can tomato sauce
1 (1.5-oz.) envelope taco seasoning
1 cup water

Drain meat of any grease; add to slow cooker with remaining ingredients, stir, cover and cook on HIGH for 4 hours, or on LOW for 7 to 8 hours. Serve hot. Goes great with cornbread or corn chips.

Makes 2 1/4 quarts.

Neal Bertrand
Lafayette, La.

Black-Eyed Pea & Sausage Soup

1 lb. smoked sausage, cut in small pieces and browned in skillet
3 strips bacon, cut into 1-inch pieces and cooked in skillet
1 (.87-oz.) package Brown Gravy Mix
2 (15.5-oz.) cans black-eyed peas with jalapenos, undrained
1 (10.5-oz.) can chicken broth
1 medium onion, chopped
3 green onions, chopped
1/2 cup (1 stalk) chopped celery
1/2 tsp. garlic powder
1/2 tsp. oregano
TABASCO® Brand Pepper Sauce to taste, or serve at the table
2 cups water, divided

Drain grease from sausage and bacon; put meat in slow cooker. Make the Brown Gravy Mix using 1 cup water according to package directions. Add remaining ingredients, stir, cover and cook on HIGH for 3 hours, or on LOW for 6 hours.

Makes about 3 quarts.

Neal Bertrand
Lafayette, La.

Chicken Noodle Soup

Here's a traditional homemade soup that is tasty and hearty.

1 lb. chicken breast or your favorite cut of chicken
Salt and pepper, to taste
1 (10 1/2-oz.) can cream of chicken soup
2 (10 1/2-oz.) cans chicken broth
1 cup baby carrots, coarsely chopped
1 stalk celery, chopped
1 small onion, chopped
3 cloves garlic, minced
1/4 cup chopped green onion
1/4 cup parsley
1/2 stick butter, chopped
5 cups water
6 oz. (half of a 12-oz. box) fettuccine noodles, broken in half, cooked on stove

Cut chicken in small pieces, brown in skillet and add seasonings. Add all ingredients to slow cooker except noodles, stir, cover and cook on LOW for 6 to 8 hours.
Makes about 2 quarts.

Steak & Potato Soup

1 lb. boneless round steak, cut into very small pieces and seasoned

1/2 tsp. Cajun or Creole seasoning

Salt, to taste

1 tbsp. butter

1/2 large onion, chopped

1/2 bell pepper, chopped

5 garlic cloves, minced

1 (.87-oz.) envelope Brown Gravy Mix made according to package directions

4 medium potatoes, (4 cups), cut into small cubes

1 (10.75-oz.) can cream of potato soup

1 (10.5-oz.) can beef broth

1 (10-oz.) can diced tomatoes with green chilies

2 tsp. Worcestershire sauce

1/8 tsp. dried bay leaf flakes

1/2 tsp. dried basil

1 pint half and half

TABASCO® Brand Pepper Sauce to taste, or serve at the table

Shredded mild cheddar cheese, as garnish

1/2 cup finely chopped green onion, as garnish

1/2 cup finely chopped parsley, as garnish

Sour cream, as garnish (optional)

Add all ingredients to slow cooker except the last six items, then stir and cover.

Cook on HIGH for 4 hours, or on LOW for 7 to 8 hours. Stir in half & half, and then serve. Use garnish items as needed.

Makes about 2 1/4 quarts.

NOTE:

Make this soup Southwestern-style by adding one-half to one can of both black beans and whole kernel corn, drained, and one-half to one teaspoon cumin. Garnish as suggested above, with the addition of avocado slices (optional).

– Contributed by Lisa Menard
Lafayette, La.

Beef Stroganoff #1

2-3 lbs. beef chuck (cut in strips or cubes)
1 can cream of chicken
1 can cream of mushroom
1 can cream of celery
1 pkg. dry French onion soup mix

Cook 4 hours on HIGH in slow cooker or until tender. Serve over noodles or rice.

Charlotte Martin
Minden, La.

Beef Stroganoff #2

2 lb. flank or round steak
Salt and pepper, to taste
1 onion, sliced
1 clove garlic, minced
1 can mushrooms, drained
2 cups beef boullion or broth
1 tbsp. ketchup
1 tbsp. Worcestershire sauce
1/4 cup dry sherry
2 tbsp. flour
2 tbsp. butter
1 cup sour cream

Slice beef into quarter-inch strips about 2-inches long. Sprinkle with salt and pepper and place in slow cooker. Mix together onion, garlic, mushrooms, beef bullion, ketchup, Worcestershire sauce and sherry. Stir into beef. Cover and cook on LOW for 6-8 hours. Set cooker on HIGH. Stir in flour and butter which have been blended together. Stir until thickened. Turn off heat. After a few minutes, stir in sour cream. Serve with rice or noodles. Serves 4-6. (Cooked in a 4-quart slow cooker.)

Nancy Unsworth
Doyline, La.

Potato Cheddar Cheese Soup

6-10 potatoes, peeled and cubed
1/2 cup vegetable broth
1 cup water
1 large onion, finely chopped
1/2 tsp. garlic powder

1/8 tsp. white pepper
2 cups milk, heated
1 cup shredded sharp or cheddar
   cheese
Paprika

Place potatoes, broth, water, onion, and garlic powder in slow cooker.
Cover and cook on LOW 7-9 hours or on HIGH for 4-6 hours.
Mash potatoes, leaving them a bit lumpy. Stir in pepper and milk a little
at a time. Add cheese. Cook until cheese has melted, about 5 minutes.
Add more milk depending if you'd like a thinner or creamier soup.
Garnish each serving with paprika.
Makes 4 servings. Cooked in a 4-quart slow cooker.

Elizabeth Lynn, MA
Assistant Extension Agent
Bienville Parish 4-H

Four Layer Stew

1st layer: fresh or frozen carrots
2nd layer: fresh or canned potatoes
3rd layer: browned hamburger
**4th layer: 1 or 2 cans each cream of mushroom, vegetable soup, or
   tomato soup**

Place in slow cooker, add seasonings of your choice, and cook several
hours until cooked. Serve with bread.

Black-Eyed Pea & Sausage Stew

1 lb. smoked link beef or pork
    sausage, sliced and browned
    (Browning optional)
1 (15.5-oz.) can black-eyed peas
    with jalapenos
1 (10.5-oz.) can beef broth
1/2 to 1 stick butter, chopped

1 small onion, chopped
1 small bell pepper, chopped
3 cloves garlic, minced
1/2 cup chopped green onions
TABASCO® Brand Pepper Sauce to
    taste, or serve at the table

Add all ingredients to slow cooker and cook on HIGH for 3 hours, or on LOW for 6 or 7 hours.
Makes 1 1/2 quarts.
Serve over hot rice or pasta.

Neal Bertrand
Lafayette, La.

Easy Stroganoff

1 lb. lean stew meat
1 can golden mushroom soup
1 can cream of chicken soup

1 can French onion soup
1 can mushrooms

Mix together and cook all day on LOW. Serve over rice. (Can use chicken breasts instead of stew meat).

Marilyn Morgan
Haynesville, La.

Meatball & Vegetable Stew

1 (16- to 18-oz.) package frozen meatballs

1/2 of a 16 oz. package (about 2 cups) loose pack frozen broccoli, corn, and red sweet peppers, or other mixed vegetables

1 (14 1/2-oz.) can diced tomatoes with onion and garlic, or stewed tomatoes, undrained

1 (12-oz.) jar mushroom gravy

1/3 cup water

1 1/2 tsp. dried basil, crushed

In a 3-1/2- or 4-quart slow cooker, place meatballs and mixed vegetables. In a bowl, stir together tomatoes, gravy, water and basil; pour over meatballs and vegetables in cooker. Cover and cook on LOW for 6 to 8 hours or on HIGH for 3 to 4 hours.
Makes 4 servings.
(For a 5 or 6 quart slow cooker: Double all ingredients. Makes 8 quarts.)

Janet Lasseigne
Parks, La.

Easy Chili

My son Steven created this recipe the traditional way on the stove when he was twelve years old. He's been wowing guests and family with it ever since. Now it has been perfected to work in your slow cooker.

1 lb. ground meat of your choice

1/4 tsp. Cajun or Creole seasoning

1/2 tsp. garlic powder

1/2 tsp. onion powder

1 (1.25-oz.) envelope Chili Seasoning Mix

1 cup water

1 (15.5-oz.) can small red chili beans in spicy tomato sauce

1 (10-oz.) can diced tomatoes with green chilis

Brown the ground meat in a skillet; drain excess grease.
Season the meat well; pour chili packet into cup of water, stir to dissolve.
Add all ingredients to slow cooker and cook on HIGH for 4 hours or on
LOW for 6 to 7 hours.

Makes one quart.

– Steven Bertrand
Lafayette, La.

Old-Fashioned Stew

1/2 cup flour
1 tsp. salt
1/8 tsp. pepper
1/8 tsp. cloves
2 lbs. beef stew meat, cut into
    1-in. cubes
3 tbsp. butter
1 large onion, chopped

1 (28-oz.) can whole tomatoes
    (undrained)
1 green pepper, cut into 1-in. pieces
1 cup water
1 beef bouillon cube
2 tbsp. cornstarch
1/4 cup cold water

In a medium bowl combine flour, salt, pepper and cloves; add beef and
coat evenly. Melt butter in skillet, add dredged meat and brown. Remove
meat from pot and put into slow cooker along with onion, tomatoes and
green pepper. Add water to meat drippings in skillet, bring to a boil, then
add bouillon cube and stir until dissolved; add to slow cooker. Cook on
HIGH for 4 hours. To thicken liquid, mix cornstarch with 1/4 cup water
and stir slowly into hot liquid. Keep warm on LOW. Makes 6 to 8 servings.

Patricia Bessinger
Caddo Parrish Volunteers for Family & Community
Southern Hills Club

Chicken & Sausage Gumbo

1 1/2 lbs. boneless chicken breast (or your favorite parts) cut in bite-size pieces
1/2 tsp. salt
1 tsp. Cajun or Creole seasoning
1 lb. smoked sausage, cut in small pieces
1/2 large (2/3 cup) bell pepper, chopped
1 small onion, chopped
3 cloves garlic, minced
1 green onion, chopped
TABASCO® Brand Pepper Sauce to taste, or serve at the table
1/2 cup Tony Chachere's Creole Instant Roux Mix
7 cups water, divided
Hot, fluffy rice

Add seasoned chicken, sausage, vegetables and seasoning to slow cooker.

To Prepare Roux Mix: In a saucepan over medium heat, whisk one-half cup Roux Mix into two cups cool water. Bring to a boil, whisking until well dissolved. After mixture begins to thicken, remove from heat, and pour into slow cooker.

Add remaining five cups water to slow cooker, stir well, cover, and cook on HIGH for 3 hours.

Serve in bowls over hot, fluffy rice. Makes 3 quarts.

Neal Bertrand
Lafayette, La.

Italian Stew

6 hot (or sweet) Italian
   sausages
1 lb. beef chuck, cut in 1-in.
   cubes
1 large onion, sliced
2 medium cloves garlic, minced
2 green peppers, seeded & cut
   in eighths

4 medium potatoes, peeled and cut in
   quarters
1 cup carrot chunks
2 cans red kidney beans, drained
1 tsp. basil
1/2 tsp. salt
1/2 tsp. pepper
1 can beef broth

In a heavy skillet, over medium heat, brown sausage well. Cut each link in thirds and place in slow cooker. Drain fat from skillet, reserving 2 tbsp. Brown beef in 1 tbsp. fat then put into pot with sausage. Cook onion and garlic in remaining tbsp. fat until tender. Add green pepper and cook 1 minute longer, stirring occasionally. Add to slow cooker along with potatoes, carrots and beans. Sprinkle with seasonings and mix lightly. Add beef broth. Cover and cook on HIGH 3 hours, or until beef, potatoes, and carrots are tender. Serves 6 to 8.

Margaret Newton
Caddo Parish Volunteers for Family & Community
Southern Hills Club

Bayou Gumbo

3 tbsp. all purpose flour
3 tbsp. oil
1/2 lb. smoked sausage, cut into 1/2-inch slices
2 cups frozen cut okra
1 large onion, chopped
1 large green bell pepper, chopped
3 garlic cloves, minced
1/4 tsp. ground red cayenne pepper
1/4 tsp. black pepper
1 (14.5-oz.) can diced tomatoes, undrained
1 (12-oz.) package frozen shelled deveined cooked medium shrimp, rinsed
1 1/2 cups uncooked regular long-grain white rice
3 cups water

In a small saucepan, make a roux by combining flour and oil; mix well. Cook, stirring constantly over medium-high heat for 5 minutes. Reduce heat to medium; cook, stirring constantly, about 10 minutes or until mixture turns reddish brown.

Place flour-oil mixture in 3 1/2- to 4-quart slow cooker. Stir in all remaining ingredients except shrimp, rice and water.

Cover; cook on LOW setting for 7-9 hours. When ready to serve, cook rice in water as directed on package. Meanwhile, add shrimp to gumbo mixture in slow cooker; mix well. Cover; cook on LOW setting for additional 20 minutes. Serve gumbo over cooked rice. Makes 6 servings.

Elsie Castille
Breaux Bridge, La.
St. Martin Parish

Corn & Potato Soup

2 (10.75-oz.) cans condensed cream of potato soup
1 lb. fresh or frozen corn
2 green onions, chopped
3 cloves garlic, minced
4 tbsp. butter
3 oz. cream cheese, room temperature, cubed
1/2 tsp. onion powder, or to taste
1/4 tsp. black pepper, or to taste
TABASCO® Brand Pepper Sauce to taste, or serve at the table
3/4 cup water
1 pint (16 oz.) half & half (light cream) or milk
Bacon bits

Add all ingredients to slow cooker except half & half and bacon bits, stir, cover and cook on low for 6 hours. Add the half & half or milk, and stir. Cover and continue cooking for 10 minutes, then serve. Add bacon bits to bowl of soup.

– Steven Bertrand
Lafayette, La.

Spicy Turkey Chili

2 (5 oz.) cans turkey meat, drained
2 (15-oz.) cans kidney beans
2 (14.5-oz.) cans Italian-style stewed tomatoes
2 (1.25-oz.) packages chili seasoning mix
1 (4-oz.) can green chili peppers
1 (8-oz.) can tomato sauce
1 onion, diced
1 cup water

In a slow cooker, combine all ingredients and cook on low 3 to 4 hours. Serve hot.

Crawfish & Corn Maque Choux Soup

1 (14.75-oz.) can sweet cream corn
1 (15.25-oz.) can whole kernel
   sweet corn, undrained
1 (10-oz.) can diced tomatoes with
   green chilies
1 onion, chopped
1 bell pepper, chopped
1 stalk celery, chopped

4 cloves garlic, minced
1/2 stick butter, chopped
1/2 tsp. Cajun or Creole seasoning
1 lb. crawfish tails, peeled and
   deveined
1 pint (2 cups) half & half (light
   cream), optional

Add all ingredients to slow cooker except last two ingredients; stir well, cover and cook on LOW for 5 hours. Add crawfish and cook on LOW for 1 hour. When done, add half & half, stir well and serve.

Makes about 3 quarts.

Neal Bertrand
Lafayette, La.

Mexican Style Chicken Stew

2 lbs. skinless, boneless chicken
   breasts cut into 1 1/2-inch pieces
4 medium russet potatoes, peeled
   and cut very small
1 (15-oz.) can mild salsa

1 (4-oz.) can diced green
   chilies
1 (1.25-oz.) package taco
   seasoning mix
1 (8-oz.) can tomato sauce

Mix all ingredients together in slow cooker and cook 7-9 hours on low. Serve with warm flour tortillas.

VEGETABLES

Red Beans & Rice

At most of the "plate lunch" places in south Louisiana, this simple but tasty dish is special enough to serve once a week. For some, nothing else is better.

1 lb. smoked beef or pork
    sausage
1 (15.5-oz.) can red beans,
    undrained
1 (15.5-oz.) can chili beans,
    undrained
5 oz. beef broth
1 bell pepper, chopped

1 onion, chopped
1 green onion, chopped
3 cloves garlic, minced
1/2 tsp. Cajun or Creole seasoning
TABASCO® Brand Pepper Sauce to
    taste, or serve at the table
1/2 cup water
Hot, cooked rice

Slice sausage in small pieces, then add all ingredients to slow cooker except rice. Stir, cover and cook on HIGH for 3 1/2 hours, or LOW for 6 or 7 hours.

Serve immediately over hot rice.

Makes 1 1/2 quarts.

Neal Bertrand
Lafayette, La.

Orange-Glazed Carrots

3 cups sliced carrots
2 cups water
1/4 tsp. salt

3 tbsp. butter
3 tbsp. orange marmalade
2 tbsp. chopped pecans

Combine carrots, water, and salt in slow cooker. Cover and cook on HIGH 2 to 3 hours or until the carrots are done. Drain well; stir in remaining ingredients. Cover and cook on HIGH 20 to 30 minutes. Makes 5 to 6 servings.

Charlotte Martin
Minden, La.

Crawfish Boil Potatoes & Corn

When we have our family crawfish boil, we always put potatoes and corn-on-the-cob into the pot along with the crawfish. I had the idea of doing the same thing in a slow cooker. It came out great the first time we tried it.

2 cups water
1 tbsp. liquid crab & shrimp
    boil
1 tsp. salt
1/2 tsp. red pepper

1/2 stick butter, chopped
3 lbs. red potatoes, cleaned well,
    unpeeled and quartered
4 ears corn on the cob
1 large onion, chopped fine

Add water and seasoning to slow cooker and stir.
Add remaining ingredients, stir, cover and cook on LOW for 6 hours.

Makes 2 1/4 quarts.

Neal Bertrand
Lafayette, La.

Chili & Cheese Stuffed Potato

This is an All-American meal, hearty enough for even the biggest appetites. A major crowd pleaser!

1 lb. ground beef or turkey, browned, drained
Salt, red & black pepper, to taste
1 tsp. chili powder
1 (1.25-oz.) envelope chili seasoning mix
1 cup water
1 (2-lb.) bag frozen, crinkle-cut French-fried potatoes, defrosted

1 (15.5-oz.) can small red beans in spicy tomato sauce (Chili Beans)
1/2 stick butter, chopped
1 medium onion, chopped
1 (8-oz.) can tomato sauce
TABASCO® Brand Pepper Sauce to taste, or serve at the table
1 (8-oz.) package shredded Monterey Jack, or your favorite cheese
Sour cream (optional)
Chopped green onion tops (optional)

Brown ground meat in skillet, season well with salt, pepper, and chili powder; add to pot. Dissolve chili seasoning mix in one cup water and add to pot.

Add remaining ingredients to slow cooker except cheese, sour cream and onion tops.

Stir and mix well, pressing down on the potatoes to coat with liquid.

Cover and cook for 4 1/2 hours on LOW.

Remove lid and stir well, which will break up the remaining unbroken potatoes.

Place a serving on plate and add cheese and mix well. Add sour cream, onion tops or any of the traditional baked potato fixings.

Makes 2 3/4 quarts.

– Neal & Steven Bertrand
Lafayette, La.

Chicken Fajita Stuffed Potato

1 lb. boneless, skinless chicken
    breast cut in small pieces
Salt, red & black pepper, to taste
1 (1.12-oz.) envelope fajita mix
6 oz. water
1 (2-lb.) bag frozen, crinkle-cut
    French-fried potatoes, defrosted

1 medium onion, chopped fine
1/2 red bell pepper, chopped fine
1/2 stick butter, chopped
5 oz. chicken broth
TABASCO® Brand Pepper Sauce
    to taste, or serve at the table

Season chicken with salt and peppers; stir.
Dissolve fajita mix in measuring cup with 6 ounces of water.
Add all ingredients to slow cooker, stir, cover and cook on HIGH for 3 hours, or on LOW for 6 hours.

Makes 1 3/4 quarts.

– Neal Bertrand
Lafayette, La.

Black-Eyed Peas

3 to 4 slices uncooked bacon,
    chopped
3 cloves garlic, minced
4 green onions, chopped
1 cup chopped, peeled fresh or
    canned tomatoes

Salt and pepper, to taste
1 tsp. dried oregano
1 cup water
1 lb. fresh or frozen black-eyed
    peas, thawed

Combine all ingredients in slow cooker. Cover and cook on HIGH 5 to 6 hours.

Candied Yams with Marshmallows

Mom and Dad made candied yams every year for our Thanksgiving family get-togethers. They cooked them in the oven. They always made them the day before then refrigerated them overnight, covered, during which time the thin syrup thickened. I remember it took them several hours to get a finished product. I converted their recipe to be cooked in a slow cooker. What a delicious dish!

2 1/2 lbs. raw yams (sweet potatoes), peeled & diced into 1/2-inch cubes
1/2 stick butter, chopped
8 oz. (1/2 bottle) light corn syrup
1 (5-oz.) can evaporated milk
Juice of 1 lemon

1/2 tsp. cinnamon
Pinch of nutmeg
2 cups large marshmallows, or to taste
1 cup chopped pecans

Add all ingredients to slow cooker except marshmallows and pecans, stir, cover and cook on HIGH for 4 1/2 hours. Once yams are cooked, add marshmallows and pecans and stir.
Cover and let it stand covered 10 minutes before serving.

Makes about 1 1/4 quarts.

Neal Bertrand
Lafayette, La.

Yams with Brown Sugar

This is a delicious dish. The yams (sweet potatoes) turned out very soft and made a brown syrup liquid which candied after refrigerating.

2 lbs. uncooked yams, peeled and
    diced in 1/2-inch cubes
1 cup brown sugar, packed
1 stick butter, chopped

1/2 cup water
1/2 tsp. cinnamon
Pinch nutmeg

Add all ingredients to slow cooker, stir, cover and cook on HIGH for 4 1/2 hours.
Makes about 1 quart.

Neal Bertrand
Lafayette, La.

Home-Style Cornbread Dressing

1 (8 1/2-oz.) package cornbread mix
8 slices day-old bread, torn
4 eggs, beaten
1 onion, chopped
1/4 cup celery, chopped
2 (10 3/4-oz.) cans cream of chicken
    soup

2 (14 1/2-oz.) cans chicken
    broth
1 1/2 tbsp. dried sage
1 tsp. salt
1/4 tsp. pepper
2 tbsp. butter, sliced

Prepare cornbread according to package directions; cool and crumble. Mix together all ingredients except butter. Pour into a lightly greased slow cooker; dot with butter. Cover and cook on LOW setting for 4 hours, or on HIGH setting for 2 hours. Makes 16 servings.

Contributed by Cathy Judd

Sausage, Potatoes & Green Beans

Supper's done! All in one pot! Call the kids! The whole family will enjoy this hearty and very tasty meal.

Note: For convenience, you may substitute a two-pound bag of frozen crinkle-cut French fried potatoes for the whole potatoes.

1 lb. smoked sausage or sirloin steak, sliced small and browned

2 lbs. (about 5 medium) potatoes, cleaned well, unpeeled and quartered

1 (14.5-oz.) can green beans with liquid

1 (10.5-oz.) can beef broth

1 medium onion, chopped

1/2 bell pepper, chopped

1/2 stick butter, chopped

Salt and pepper, to taste

Onion and garlic powder, to taste

1 cup water

Brown meat in skillet. Drain grease. Add all ingredients to slow cooker, stir, cover and cook on HIGH for 3 hours, or on LOW for 6 or 7 hours.

Makes 2 1/4 quarts.

Neal Bertrand
Lafayette, La.

Baked Beans

1 lb. bacon

1 large onion, chopped

2 cans Great Northern beans, drained

2 cans kidney beans, drained

2 cans pork & beans in tomato sauce

1 cup ketchup

2 tbsp. Worcestershire sauce

3/4 cup brown sugar

Cheddar cheese

Cook bacon until crispy, then crumble. Mix all together in slow cooker except cheese. Cook on HIGH for 2 hours, then on LOW for 6 hours. When ready to serve, sprinkle cheese on top.

DESSERTS

Carrot Cake #1

1 (18.25-oz.) box spice cake mix
1 (3.4-oz.) box instant French
  vanilla pudding mix
1 cup water
3/4 cup canola oil
4 eggs

4 (3.5-oz.) packs pureed carrots
  – (found in baby food section,
  2nd stage)
1 (8-oz.) can crushed pineapple
1 cup sour cream

Spray a 5-quart slow cooker with no-stick canola oil cooking spray (or use the slow cooker liners).
Combine all ingredients in a large mixing bowl. Beat with an electric mixer on medium speed for 2 minutes. Slowly pour into slow cooker. Take 2 full size paper towel sheets and place on top of cooker, then put lid on*. Cook on LOW for 4 to 5 1/2 hours, depending on your slow cooker. When done, spoon out while warm and serve with some vanilla ice cream!

* The paper towel will absorb the moisture build-up in your slow cooker and keep the cake from being soggy.

Kathy Mauthe, Extension Agent, Tangipahoa Parish
LSU AgCenter
Amite, La.

Triple Chocolate Cake

18 1/2-oz. package chocolate
  cake mix
8 oz. sour cream
3.4-oz. package instant
  chocolate pudding mix

12 oz. package chocolate chips
4 eggs, beaten
3/4 cup oil
1 cup water
Vanilla ice cream, optional

Place all ingredients except ice cream in a slow cooker; mix well. Cover and cook on HIGH for 3 hours. If desired, serve with ice cream.
Makes 8 to 10 servings.

Contributed by Cynthia Stephens

Applesauce Spice Cake

1/4 cup butter
1/2 cup sugar
1 egg
1/2 tsp. vanilla
3/4 cup applesauce
1 cup flour

1 tsp. baking soda
1/4 tsp. ground cloves
1/4 tsp. nutmeg
1/2 cup raisins (optional)
1/2 cup chopped walnuts (optional)

Cream the butter and sugar. Add egg and vanilla and beat well. Beat in applesauce. In another bowl combine flour, baking soda and spices and stir into creamed mixture. Blend in raisins and nuts. Pour into greased and floured Bread'n Cake Bake pan and cover. Place in slow cooker, cover and bake on HIGH 2½ to 4 hours.

Carrot Cake #2

2 eggs
1 cup sugar
2/3 cup oil
1 1/2 cups flour
1 tsp. baking soda

1/2 tsp. salt
1 tsp. vanilla
1 tsp. cinnamon
3/4 cup grated carrots
1/2 cup chopped nuts

Beat together the eggs, sugar, and oil. In another bowl combine the flour, baking soda, salt, vanilla, and cinnamon and add to the sugar mixture and beat well. Stir in the carrots and nuts. Pour into a greased and floured Bread'n Cake Bake pan. Cover and place in the slow cooker. Cover and bake on HIGH for 2 1/2 to 4 hours.

Bananas Foster

6 bananas, peeled and cut in quarters
1/2 cup flaked coconut
1/2 tsp. cinnamon
1/4 tsp. salt
1/2 cup dark corn syrup
1/3 cup unsalted butter, melted
1 tsp. lemon zest, grated
3 tbsp. lemon juice
1 tsp. rum
12 slices pound cake
1 quart French vanilla ice cream, softened
Powdered sugar, for garnish

Combine the bananas and coconut in the slow cooker. In a medium mixing bowl, combine the cinnamon, salt, corn syrup, butter, lemon zest, lemon juice, and rum. Pour over the banana and coconut mixture. Cover and cook on LOW for 1-2 hours. To create individual servings, place one scoop of the ice cream between two slices of pound cake. Ladle the bananas and sauce over each ice cream sandwich and dust with powdered sugar.

Peach Cobbler

2 lbs. fresh or canned peaches, sliced
2/3 cup oats (oatmeal)
2/3 cup flour
2/3 cup light brown sugar
1/2 tsp. ground cinnamon
1/4 tsp. nutmeg
3/4 cup softened butter

If using canned peaches, drain liquid and place in the slow cooker. In a small bowl, combine oats, flour, brown sugar, cinnamon, and nutmeg and pour over the peaches. Add the butter and stir until crumbly. Cook on LOW for 3 hours.

Nutty Chocolate Fudge

3 (8-oz.) packages dark melting chocolate
4 (6-oz.) packages white melting chocolate
4 oz. sweet baking chocolate, chopped
12 oz. semi-sweet chocolate chips
2 (12-oz.) jars salted peanuts

Place dark chocolate, white chocolate and sweet chocolate in a slow cooker; cover and cook on LOW setting until melted. Add chocolate chips and peanuts; continue to cook, covered, on LOW setting. Stir; cover, and cook for an additional hour. Stir again and cook for an additional hour. Drop by tablespoonfuls onto wax paper; cool completely. Store in an airtight container for up to 3 months. Makes about 4 dozen pieces.

Pear Crunch

1 (8-oz.) can crushed pineapple in juice, undrained
1/4 cup pineapple or apple juice
3 tbsp. dried cranberries
1 1/2 tsp. quick-cooking tapioca
1/4 tsp. vanilla
2 pears, cored and cut into halves
1/4 cup granola with almonds

Combine all ingredients except pears and granola in slow cooker and mix well. Place pears, cut side down, over pineapple mixture. Cover and cook on LOW 3 1/2 to 4 1/2 hours. Arrange pear halves on serving plates. Spoon pineapple mixture over pear halves. Garnish with granola.

Rocky Road Cake

1 (18.25-oz.) package German chocolate cake mix

1 (3.9-oz.) package instant chocolate pudding mix

3 large eggs, slightly beaten

1 cup sour cream

1/3 cup butter, melted

1 tsp. vanilla

3 1/4 cup milk, divided: 1 1/4 and 2 cup divisions

1 (3.4-oz.) package chocolate cook-and-serve pudding mix

1/2 cup chopped pecans

1 1/2 cup mini marshmallows

1 cup semi-sweet chocolate chips

Beat cake mix with next 5 ingredients plus 1 1/4 cup milk with an electric mixer for 2 minutes, scraping down the sides of the bowl as needed.

Pour batter into lightly greased 4 qt. slow cooker (I used 6 qt. and slightly less cooking time).

Heat remaining 2 cups milk in non-aluminum saucepan, heating and stirring just until scalded.

Sprinkle cook-and-serve pudding over the batter and slowly pour hot milk over the pudding.

Cover and cook on LOW 3 1/2 hours. Meanwhile, heat chopped pecans in a small nonstick skillet on medium-low heat, 3 to 5 minutes until lightly toasted and fragrant.

Turn off slow cooker when time is up, or when cake seems set and not soupy or jiggly.

Sprinkle cake with pecans, marshmallows and chocolate chips. Let stand 15 minutes or until marshmallows are slightly melted. Serve warm with ice cream.

Makes 12 large servings or possibly 18-20 smaller "just right" servings.

Contributed by Deniese L. Zeringue
LSU AgCenter

Apple Pie

8 tart apples, peeled and sliced
1 1/4 tsp. ground cinnamon
1/4 tsp. allspice
1/4 tsp. nutmeg
3/4 cup milk
2 tbsp. butter, softened
3/4 cup sugar

2 eggs
1 tsp. vanilla
1 1/2 cups Bisquick, divided
1/3 cup brown sugar
3 tbsp. cold butter

Toss apples in large bowl with cinnamon, allspice, and nutmeg. Place in slow cooker. In a bowl, combine milk, softened butter, sugar, eggs, vanilla, and 1/2 cup Bisquick. Spoon over apples. Combine 1 cup Bisquick and brown sugar. Cut the cold butter into mixture until crumbly. Sprinkle this mixture over top of apple mixture. Cover and cook on LOW 6-7 hours or until apples are soft.

Banana Nut Bread

1/3 cup shortening
1/2 cup sugar
2 eggs
1 3/4 cup all purpose flour
1 tsp. baking powder

1/2 tsp. baking soda
1/2 tsp. salt
1 cup mashed ripe bananas
1/2 cup chopped walnuts

Cream together shortening and sugar; add eggs and beat well. Sift dry ingredients; add to creamed mixture alternately with banana, blending well after each addition. Stir in nuts. Pour into well-greased 4 to 6 cup mold, such as a ceramic soufflé dish. Cover with foil and tie a string tightly around it to keep foil down. Pour 2 cups hot water in slow cooker. Place mold on metal veggie steamer rack or trivet in pot. Cover and cook on HIGH 2 to 3 hours or until bread is done. Be sure not to check bread during the first 2 hours of cooking.

Peanut Clusters

1 (16-oz.) jar unsalted dry
   roasted peanuts
1 (16-oz.) jar salted roasted
   peanuts
1 (12-oz.) package semi-sweet
   chocolate (broken into
   smaller pieces)

1 (4-oz.) bar German sweet
   chocolate (broken into smaller
   pieces)
3 lbs. (or 2 planks) white chocolate
   bark

Place ingredients into slow cooker in the order given. Cover the pot and cook on LOW heat for 3 hours. DO NOT REMOVE THE LID. When done, stir until thoroughly mixed. You may then drop by teaspoonfuls onto waxed paper. Should make about 170 pieces.

HINT: I line a large cookie sheet with parchment paper and pour the candy onto it. After it has set (approximately 2 hours), I cut it into square pieces using a pizza cutter. This is much faster, but of course the dropped one is prettier. (Cooked in a 5-quart slow cooker.)

Sylvia Guillotte
Jennings, La.

Spicy Pecans

1/4 cup (4 oz.) butter, cut in pieces
6 cups pecans
2 tsp. chili powder

1/2 tsp. onion salt
1/2 tsp. garlic powder

Place butter in slow cooker; heat, uncovered, on HIGH until melted, about 15 minutes. Add pecans; stir to coat. Cover and cook on HIGH 30 minutes. Uncover and cook on HIGH 2 1/2 hours longer, stirring occasionally. Sprinkle with the seasonings and toss to coat. Spread on a baking sheet to cool. Can be stored in an airtight container in the refrigerator for 4 to 6 weeks.

Coconut Rice Pudding

2 3/4 cups water
3/4 cup long-grain white rice
1 (15-oz.) can cream of coconut
   (not coconut milk)
1 (12-oz.) can evaporated milk

2/3 cup sweetened flaked coconut
   (optional)
1 tbsp. dark rum (optional)

In a 4 1/2 to 6 quart slow cooker bowl, stir water, rice, cream of coconut, and evaporated milk until combined. Cover slow cooker with lid and cook as manufacturer directs on LOW setting 4 to 5 hours or on HIGH for 2½ to 3 hours. If you like, while pudding cooks, toast coconut: Heat nonstick small skillet over medium heat until hot. Add coconut; cook 4 to 5 minutes or until lightly browned, stirring constantly. Transfer coconut to plate. Remove bowl from slow cooker. Stir in rum, if using. Let pudding stand 10 minutes. Transfer pudding to serving bowl. If not serving right away, press sheet of plastic wrap onto pudding; refrigerate up to 2 days. To serve, spoon pudding into dessert bowls; sprinkle with toasted coconut, if using. Makes about 10 half-cup servings.

Sugared & Spiced Pecans or Walnuts

16 oz. pecans or walnut halves
1/2 cup melted unsalted butter
1/2 cup powdered sugar

1/4 tsp. ground cloves
1 1/2 tsp. ground cinnamon
1/4 tsp. ground ginger

Turn slow cooker to HIGH about 15 minutes in advance. In hot slow cooker, stir together the nuts and butter. Add the powdered sugar, stirring to blend and coat evenly. Cover and cook on HIGH for 15 minutes. Reduce the heat to LOW and remove lid; cook, uncovered, stirring occasionally, for about 2 to 3 hours, or until the nuts are coated with a crisp glaze. Transfer the nuts to a bowl. In another small bowl, combine the spices; sift over the nuts, stirring to coat evenly. Let cool before serving.

Cherry Cobbler

1 (16-oz.) can cherry pie filling
1 package cake mix for one layer cake
1 egg

3 tbsp. evaporated milk
1/2 tsp. cinnamon

Put pie filling in lightly buttered 3 1/2 quart slow cooker and cook on HIGH for 30 minutes. Mix together the remaining ingredients and spoon onto the hot pie filling. Cover and cook for 2-3 hours on LOW. If you use a larger slow cooker, put all ingredients into a lightly greased soufflé dish. Makes 6 servings.

Chocolate Pudding Cake

1 cup Bisquick® biscuit mix
1 cup granulated sugar, divided
3 tbsp. plus 1/3 cup unsweetened
    cocoa

1/2 cup milk
1 tsp. vanilla extract
1 2/3 cup hot water

Mix Bisquick, 1/2 cup of the sugar, the 3 tablespoons cocoa, milk and vanilla extract. Spoon batter evenly into a greased slow cooker.
Mix remaining sugar, cocoa and hot water.
Pour over batter in slow cooker. Cook on HIGH for 2 to 2 1/2 hours, or until batter no longer looks shiny on top. Don't overcook. The batter rises to the top like cake, and underneath is a rich chocolate pudding.
Serve with ice cream or whipped cream.

ABOUT THE AUTHOR

Neal Bertrand was born and reared in Opelousas, Louisiana, USA, in the heart of Cajun Country. He has more than a decade of experience in the publishing business. He is the founder and owner of Cypress Cove Publishing in Lafayette, Louisiana.

His three cookbooks are available in paperback and e-book formats:
Down-Home Cajun Cooking Favorites,
Rice Cooker Meals: Fast Home Cooking for Busy People,
Slow Cooker Meals: Easy Home Cooking for Busy People,
and the bilingual English and French *Cajun Country Fun Coloring & Activity Book* in paperback only.

INDEX

SEAFOOD

Cajun Shrimp Creole, 48
Catfish Sauce Piquante, 53
Crawfish & Corn Maque Choux, 48
Crawfish Étouffée, 49
Crawfish Jambalaya Stew, 51
Crawfish Stew, 50
Salmon with Caramelized Onions &
    Carrots, 51
Shrimp Creole, 54
Shrimp Creole Jambalaya Stew, 52
Shrimp Marinara, 54

SOUPS, STEWS & CHILI

Bayou Gumbo, 70
Beef Stroganoff #1, 63
Beef Stroganoff #2, 63
Black-Eyed Pea & Sausage Soup, 60
Black-Eyed Pea & Sausage Stew, 65
Chicken & Sausage Gumbo, 68
Chicken & White Bean Stew, 56
Chicken Noodle Soup, 61
Corn & Potato Soup, 71
Crawfish & Corn Maque
    Choux Soup, 72
Cream Cheese Potato Soup, 56
Easy Chili, 66
Easy Stroganoff, 65
Four Layer Stew, 64
Ham & Potato Chowder, 58
Italian Stew, 69
Meatball & Vegetable Stew, 66
Meatball Mushroom Soup, 57
Mexican Style Chicken Stew, 72
Navy Bean Soup, 59
Old-Fashioned Stew, 67
Potato Cheddar Cheese Soup, 64
Spicy Turkey Chili, 71
Steak & Potato Soup, 62
Taco Soup #1, 58

Taco Soup #2, 59
Taco Soup #3, 60

VEGETABLES

Baked Beans, 80
Black-Eyed Peas, 77
Candied Yams with
    Marshmallows, 78
Chicken Fajita Stuffed Potato, 77
Chili & Cheese Stuffed Potato, 76
Crawfish Boil Potatoes & Corn, 75
Home-Style Cornbread
    Dressing, 79
Orange-Glazed Carrots, 75
Red Beans & Rice, 74
Sausage, Potatoes &
    Green Beans, 80
Yams with Brown Sugar, 79

DESSERTS

Apple Pie, 87
Applesauce Spice Cake, 83
Banana Nut Bread, 87
Bananas Foster, 84
Carrot Cake #1, 82
Carrot Cake #2, 83
Cherry Cobbler, 90
Chocolate Pudding Cake, 90
Coconut Rice Pudding, 89
Nutty Chocolate Fudge, 85
Peach Cobbler, 84
Peanut Clusters, 88
Pear Crunch, 85
Rocky Road Cake, 86
Spicy Pecans, 88
Sugared & Spiced Pecans
    or Walnuts, 89
Triple Chocolate Cake, 82

Our Cookbooks are Available in Paperback and Ebook Formats

DOWN-HOME CAJUN COOKING FAVORITES, REVISED SECOND EDITION

Now even better! A collection of classic recipes from the south Louisiana region called Acadiana, or Cajun Country. They were contributed by area folks who are tremendous cooks in their own right, who learned how to cook these dishes passed down from generation to generation. You'll find a variety of sauce piquantes, fricassees, stews, casseroles, appetizers, desserts, dressings, breads and breakfast dishes like *couche-couche* and *pain perdu.* Written in clear, easy-to-follow steps. Go ahead, try them, and you, too, will cook like a Cajun!
140 Recipes, 100 Pages

SLOW COOKER MEALS: EASY HOME COOKING FOR BUSY PEOPLE

Preparing a home-cooked meal in your slow cooker is delicious, nutritious, economical and easy. Start it cooking before you leave in the morning and it's cooked when you return. Loaded with easy meals anyone can prepare, this cookbook includes Cajun meals such as jambalayas & pastalayas, sauce piquantes, étouffées, plus a large variety of soups, stews, and gumbos. It has poultry and meat dishes such as brisket, roasts, ribs and Cajun Pepper Steak. It has classics like chili and meat loaf. Also includes 17 desserts such as cobblers, puddings, fudge, peanut clusters and chocolate cake.
127 Recipes, 94 Pages

RICE COOKER MEALS: FAST HOME COOKING FOR BUSY PEOPLE

Fast, easy meals you can cook in a rice cooker; most have a 30-minute cook time. Convenient one-pot cooking means less mess to clean, easier to have good home cooking; less expensive and healthier than "fast-food". Great for busy people, college students, tailgating parties, campers/RVers, etc. Has 60 recipes to cook delicious pastas, seafood, soups, potatoes, cabbage, sweet potatoes, jambalayas and rice side dishes. Includes Mexican, Italian, Tex-Mex and Cajun recipes.
60 Recipes, 92 Pages